The Saints
MISCELLANY

HISTORY, TRIVIA, FACTS & STATS

The Saints
MISCELLANY

HISTORY, TRIVIA, FACTS & STATS

GRAHAM HILEY

The Saints
MISCELLANY
HISTORY, TRIVIA, FACTS & STATS

All statistics, facts and figures are correct as of 1st August 2008

© Graham Hiley

Graham Hiley has asserted his rights in accordance with the Copyright, Designs and Patents Act 1988 to be identified as the author of this work.

Published By:
Pitch Publishing (Brighton) Ltd
A2 Yeoman Gate
Yeoman Way
Durrington
BN13 3QZ

Email: info@pitchpublishing.co.uk
Web: www.pitchpublishing.co.uk

First published 2008

A catalogue record for this book is available from the British Library.

10-digit ISBN: 1-9054111-4-6
13-digit ISBN: 978-1-9054111-4-6

Printed and bound in Great Britain by Cromwell Press

To Theresa,
with love now and always

FOREWORD BY MATT LE TISSIER

I was delighted to be asked to write the foreword for this book – until I read the bit about my penalty record. I must admit I had never bothered to count them up but I was always under the impression I had scored 48 out of 49. It turns out that I only got 47 out of 48! And then, having robbed me of a goal, Graham Hiley expects me to write nice things about his book!

But that is the beauty of a work like this. It is packed with interesting facts and figures and things I did not know – even about myself! And, in fairness, if Graham says it is right then I believe him. After all, journalists never get anything wrong!

The beauty of this Miscellany is that you can dip in and out of it for as little or as long as you like…which is ideal for someone with my powers of concentration! It is easy to read and builds up into an entertaining look at a club which has always been very special to me. It was fascinating to read about the games and the players from before I was born – as well as all those I was involved with.

I have been fortunate to play alongside some great players and in some fantastic matches and this book has brought back a lot of magical memories of my hat-tricks, my internationals – and, apparently, my 47 successful penalties! I just hope Francis Benali has not had a goal chalked off too!

But I can firmly recommend this book as a hugely enjoyable and informative read. It makes the ideal present for any Saints fan – at least until I get round to writing my autobiography!

Matthew Le Tissier,
Southampton FC 1986-2002

INTRODUCTION

Southampton is a club where the facts are often stranger than fiction but it was still a real eye-opener writing this book which contains a whole range of statistics and background information.

The task was made much easier by the thorough research already done by club historians Duncan Holley, David Bull, Dave Juson and Gary Chalk. Their vast tome *In That Number* is essential reading for any true Saints fan or for anyone wanting to learn about the club. I am enormously indebted to them for their work which was invaluable in writing this Miscellany – although some of their research will have been based on my own work during my days at the *Southern Daily Echo*, recycling at its best! *The Echo* has also been an important point of reference for this work as has Nick Illingsworth's *Saints Preserved A–Z*.

Thanks must also go to the publishers, Pitch Publishing, editor Dan Tester and to Southampton Football Club for their co-operation and access to the picture library – and to the club's Head of Retail Leighton Mitchell who is going to sell hundreds of copies for us!

But most of all I must say a heartfelt thank you to my family and my parents for their love and support. My wonderful wife Theresa has been a fantastic friend for the past 25 years and fully deserves her signed copy of this book as a Silver Wedding anniversary present! My eldest son Martin has kept my feet firmly on the ground by telling me the "Saints Miscellany" would have been better titled "Saints won't sell any" while my daughter Catherine is a constant reminder that football is less important than watching a re-run of *The Waltons* with a bag of chocolate raisins! Special thanks go to my youngest son Tim for proofreading and pointing out way too many typing mistakes.

And of course thanks to all the players, staff, management and supporters. It is their stories which make this book so fascinating and which form the heart and soul of this great club.

Graham Hiley, 2008

PRUTTON NO PUSH-OVER

Off the field David Prutton is one of the nicest people you could wish to meet – courteous, warm, witty and ready to help anyone, giving up hours of his own time to community projects. And a decent player to boot. Yet the £2m signing from Nottingham Forest is remembered most for one moment of madness which cost him and Saints dear during a home game against Arsenal in February 2005. The fiercely competitive midfielder had already been booked when he went flying in to tackle Robert Pires with a challenge which deserved a red card in its own right. He should probably have counted himself fortunate that Alan Wiley only showed a second yellow – but by then the red mist had descended. Trying to get to the linesman to argue a point, Prutton found his way blocked by the referee – and pushed him furiously. Not surprisingly he was hauled before the FA and handed a hefty 10-match ban and a £6,000 fine. That sidelined him for virtually the rest of the season while Southampton fought for their Premiership lives. He eventually returned for the final game of the season but was unable to prevent his side being relegated as they went down 2-1 at home to Manchester United.

FROZEN WASTE

A sudden cold snap wiped out almost the entire FA Cup fourth round programme in January 1996 including Saints' home tie against Crewe – even though The Dell was perfectly playable! The pitch had been covered and the surface was passed fit by the referee only for the game to be called off by the club's safety officer. Sub-zero temperatures had left the pipes frozen – including all the toilets and the fire hose pipes. Although, if there had been a fire and there were 15,000 fans dying for a pee, they could surely have put it out themselves! When the tie was eventually played, Saints needed a Matthew Le Tissier curler to salvage a 1-1 draw from a pulsating game. The replay saw Southampton race into a 3-0 interval lead with goals by Neil Shipperley, Richard Hall and Jason Dodd. But the Railwaymen pulled it back to 3-2 and hit a post in a grandstand finale with Saints clinging on for a narrow win.

JEEPERS KEEPER

On their way to promotion to the top-flight in the 1965-66 season, Saints romped to a 9-3 win over Wolves at The Dell. But manager Ted Bates must have seen something in goalkeeper Dave MacLaren as he signed him less than a year later for the princely sum of £5,000. The Scot – whose three brothers also became professional goalkeepers – made 26 appearances for Southampton before moving to the Far East where he coached Malaysia to the finals of the Munich Olympic Games in 1972. According to Terry Paine, his talents included being able to flip a coin into his top pocket with his big toe and the ability to balance a cardboard box on his nose.

PARTY POOPERS

Saints were the last visiting team to play at Maine Road before Manchester City's famous old ground was demolished ahead of their move to the new Eastlands Stadium. There was a carnival atmosphere despite the driving rain which soaked the 1,000 Saints fans shivering in a temporary and uncovered stand. City were later fined for not giving the south coast club their full allocation of tickets, such was the demand from City supporters to see the final game at their home ground. Gordon Strachan's side spoiled the party with a 1-0 win thanks to a goal by Michael Svensson. It lifted Saints to a finishing place of eighth – and earned £1.5m more in prize money than they would have received if they had lost.

WELCOME TO DIVISION 2

After Saints won promotion to Division Two in 1960, their first two home games at the higher level were against Liverpool and Pompey. They opened with a 1-0 defeat at Rotherham but then swept aside the Merseysiders 4-1 at The Dell with goals by Terry Paine, Derek Reeves, Gerry O'Brien and John Sydenham. They then enjoyed their first local derby with Pompey for 33 years – and triumphed 5-1 with goals by Paine, O'Brien, Tommy Mulgrew, Cliff Huxford and an own goal. Saints finished the season in a creditable eighth place while Portsmouth were relegated to Division Three.

WISE TO WAIT

Dennis Wise had to wait 22 years to make his Saints debut. The midfield dynamo signed apprentice forms at Southampton in July 1983 – and eventually played for the first-team when he came off the bench in a 0-0 draw at home to Wolves in August 2005. Wise was offered a professional contract at the end of his apprenticeship but turned it down, eventually signing for Wimbledon in March 1985. He helped them to win the FA Cup in 1988 and then moved to Chelsea, Leicester and Millwall before eventually re-joining Southampton in July 2005. Things were a little different by the time he returned. In the interim Saints had changed manager 12 times and moved to a new stadium! It was a short stay though as Wise left the club in December 2005 after being passed over for the manager's job following a brief stint as caretaker boss in tandem with Dave Bassett. Wise's wait to make his debut eclipsed that of Kevin Phillips who was released as an apprentice in the summer of 1991 – and who re-signed for the club for £3.25m in August 2003. He had a mere 12 years to wait for his Saints debut. He was mainly used as a full-back during his time at The Dell but was felt to be too slight to be a defender. He signed for non-league Baldock Town who stuck him up front as an emergency striker during an injury crisis – and he never looked back. He began hitting the net regularly prompting Watford to take a £10,000 gamble and he repaid them with 24 goals in 59 league games before Sunderland splashed out £325,000 for the pint-sized poacher. He became a huge hero in the north-east netting a phenomenal 115 goals in 209 league appearances before returning to the south coast for 10 times the amount Sunderland had paid for him.

PHYSIO – HEAL THYSELF

Saints physio Jim Joyce needed treatment himself after racing onto the field to treat Nathan Dyer during the 2-1 defeat at Plymouth in January 2006. The fitness fanatic and keen runner was halfway across the pitch when he pulled up sharply with a torn hamstring – much to the amusement of the travelling fans who chanted his name as he hobbled round the touchline.

YOUNG LIONS

Saints have staged five England under-21 internationals - and each time they have had a player involved. Graham Baker captained the side in 1980 as England beat Norway 3-0 at The Dell and Danny Wallace featured in a 2-0 win over Finland four years later. His younger brother Rodney started in a 3-1 win over Hungary in 1990 under the charge of Lawrie McMenemy who had just been appointed as England assistant manager. Alan Shearer and Jason Dodd were also part of the squad but neither of them featured. James Beattie wore an England shirt for the first time as England beat Poland 5-0 at The Dell in 1999. That game attracted a capacity crowd of 15,202 - a figure which more than doubled for the full house at St Mary's when Stuart Pearce's England side beat the Republic of Ireland 3-0 in a European Championship qualifier in February 2008. Andrew Surman came off the bench for the final five minutes.

SO CLOSE

Saints looked set to reach the top-flight for the first time in their history when they led Division Two by eight points in April 1949. With just two points for a win in those days, they seemed set to claim one of the two promotion slots after a 1-0 victory at Tottenham left them eight points clear of both Fulham and West Brom. However they suffered an alarming slide losing three of their next four games and then drawing 0-0 at home to Grimsby before West Brom came to The Dell for what was effectively a sudden-death decider in the penultimate fixture. A late goal from Eric Day salvaged a 1-1 draw for Saints but their fate was no longer in their own hands. Although three points behind, Albion had two games in hand. Saints lost their final fixture 1-0 at Chesterfield while the Midlands side won their remaining games to nick the final promotion place by a point.

Division Two

	P	W	D	L	F	A	Pts
Fulham	42	24	9	9	77	37	57
West Bromwich Albion	42	24	8	10	69	39	56
Southampton	42	23	9	10	69	36	55

EVEN CLOSER

Saints missed out on promotion to the top-flight again in 1950. Having let slip an eight-point lead in 1949 to dip out by a point, they suffered even greater agony 12 months on. In those days teams finishing level on points were split not by goal difference, but by goal average where the number of goals scored was divided by the number conceded. The two Sheffield clubs and Southampton all finished joint second with 52 points from 42 games but it was Wednesday with a goal average of 1.398 who joined Spurs in Division One ahead of Sheffield United (1.387) and Saints in fourth with 1.333. But it was agonisingly close. In their final game of the campaign, Saints needed to beat West Ham 3-0 in order to secure automatic promotion and were rocked when the visitors scored twice midway through the first half. It meant Sid Cann's side now needed to score seven. They got two from Ernie Jones ands another from Ernie Stevenson to win the game but it was not enough to pip the Owls. Incidentally, under current rules The Blades would just have nicked it from their local rivals by virtue of goals scored as their goal differences were the same. Saints would still have finished fourth.

Division Two

	P	W	D	L	F	A	P
Tottenham Hotspur	42	27	7	8	81	35	61
Sheffield Wednesday	42	18	16	8	67	48	52
Sheffield United	42	19	14	9	68	49	52
Southampton	42	19	14	9	64	48	52
Leeds United	42	17	13	12	54	45	47

LEAGUE CUP BOW

Saints made their first appearance in League Cup in October 1960 when they drew 2-2 at Newport County in the first round. The sides drew 2-2 again in the replay and vice chairman John Barber won the toss of a coin for the right to stage the second replay at The Dell. The goal-fest continued with Saints trailing 3-1 after 55 minutes but they hit back to win 5-3. Southampton eventually went out in the fifth round, losing 4-2 at home to League Champions Burnley.

CITY LIMITS

Saints qualified for Europe for the first time in 1969, thanks to a bizarre ruling. In those days only one club from each city was allowed into the Fairs Cup so although Ted Bates' side finished seventh, they sneaked in because Chelsea (5th) and Spurs (6th) lost out to Arsenal in fourth spot. They still had to face a nervous wait as a proposed rule change was debated in Budapest at a meeting of the Fairs Cup (now the UEFA Cup) committee. The suggestion to scrap the one city, one club rule failed to get the necessary two thirds majority and Saints were in Europe!

GET SENT TO COVENTRY

Saints v Coventry might not sound like the type of game to appeal to many neutrals but twice in three seasons it produced 10 goals. In May 1982 the Sky Blues came to The Dell for what was expected to be a largely uneventful end-of-season encounter – but it turned into a 5-5 thriller. Saints trailed 1-0 and 2-1 in the first half but pulled level both times through Kevin Keegan and Keith Cassells. They then went 4-2 down but again fought back with 25-yard shots from Alan Ball and Cassells before Keegan fired Lawrie McMenemy's side in front for the first time with seven minutes remaining. However Mark Hateley grabbed an equaliser in the dying seconds to leave a bemused Danny Wallace thinking his side had lost 5-4 as he walked off the pitch. The following season's clash brought a comparatively tame 1-1 draw but it all kicked off again in April 1984 when Saints thumped the Sky Blues 8-2 with hat-tricks from Steve Moran and Danny Wallace plus strikes from David Armstrong and Frank Worthington. It was the first time since November 1964 that two Saints players had scored hat-tricks in the same game and left a tussle for the prized matchball. Moran gave way graciously to allow Wallace to claim his first and only hat-trick ball.

DRIVING FORCE

Bobby Stokes' winner for Saints in the 1976 FA Cup Final earned him a sponsors' car – but unfortunately he was unable to drive!

TOP RANK DEAL

Saints' first shirt sponsors were Rank Xerox who signed up in September 1980. They were followed by Air Florida for the 83-84 campaign, then Draper Tools who backed the club from 1984 to 1993 when Dimplex took over for two years. Sanderson stepped in during 1995 for four years until Friends Provident came on board just ahead of the move to the new stadium, a deal which included naming rights. Initially it was planned to call it the Friends Provident Stadium but after uproar among the fans, it was changed to reflect the club's heritage becoming the Friends Provident St Mary's Stadium. When low-cost airline Flybe took it on in 2006, the deal was simply to sponsor the shirts so the ground reverted to the St Mary's Stadium.

DRYDEN DUSTED

Richard Dryden was a bargain buy from Bristol City when he was signed by Graeme Souness for just £60,000 in July 1996. Regarded by many as a journeyman, the determined defender surprised everyone by establishing himself in the Southampton side, making 29 appearances in his first season with the club. Strong in the air and uncompromising in the tackle, the centre-back soon made the doubters eat their words – none more so than television pundit Mark Lawrenson. At the time he was presenting a football show for HTV, the regional West Country ITV station which covered Bristol City. When Dryden signed for Saints Lawrenson pledged to present the show naked if Dryden was still in the Southampton side for the final game of the season. He was – and he didn't!

FIRST FAILURE

The first time Saints lost a competitive penalty shoot-out was a League Cup fourth round tie at Bolton in November 2001. After a 2-2 draw in extra-time, it went to penalties and Marian Pahars, James Beattie, Jason Dodd, Paul Telfer and goalkeeper Paul Jones all netted to take it to sudden-death. Chirs Marsden saw his effort saved and former Saints striker Rod Wallace scored to give the home side victory.

DUTCH TREAT

Usually when clubs go on pre-season tours, they return with an assortment of mementos such as vases, plates or meaningless trophies. But when Saints went to Holland in August 1994, they came back with a player – and what a player! As they booked into their training camp just outside Arnhem, Saints found that Barcelona were also staying there for one more night. At the time the Spanish giants were managed by Johann Cruyff, a close pal of then Southampton boss Alan Ball. The pair had dinner together and during the conversation, Bally jokingly asked: "I don't suppose you have got any spare players you could let us have?" When he went down for breakfast next morning, the Barca team had already checked out – but had left behind a Danish midfielder by the name of Ronnie Ekelund. Cruyff left a message for Ball saying: "Take a look at him, see if you like him – and if you do, he's yours!" From the first moment a somewhat bemused Ekelund trained with the Southampton players, it was clear he was a class act. He played in the pre-season friendlies, scoring in a 6-1 win against part-timer Nuenen and striking up an instant rapport with Matthew Le Tissier. Ekelund promptly signed on loan with a view to a permanent move – and was an instant hit with fans and team-mates alike. His movement on and off the ball, close control, pace, vision and ability to pick out a pass transformed the side and provided the perfect foil for Le Tissier. The pair were very much on the same wavelength and between them, they ripped through the opposition in breath-taking fashion with Ekelund scoring five times in 17 starts and setting up even more for others. Saints supporters were stunned that they had managed to acquire such a talent so easily – and sadly it was too good to last. Ekelund was carrying a back injury which the club felt needed surgery. They would still have signed him on that basis but the Dane felt an operation was not necessary and the deal foundered. He went back to Spain but prolonged rest failed to cure the problem and he ended up moving back to Denmark to play for Lyngby and Odensa. He linked up again with Ball for a brief loan spell at Man City in 1995 and also had trials at Coventry, Wolves and Everton but was never quite the same player again. He briefly signed for Ray Graydon's Walsall and finished his career in the States with the San Jose Earthquakes, making a special trip back to play in Le Tissier's testimonial at St Mary's.

RONNIE EKELUND

GINGER GENIUS

Southampton media knew they were in for a rough ride from the moment Gordon Strachan walked into the press conference to confirm his appointment as manager. Midlands media, well experienced in dealing with the unpredictable firebrand, had sent advance warning to think through any questions and not ask anything obvious. But one local radio reporter was so desperate to be first to welcome the new manager live on air that he forgot the ginger rule. He began: "Welcome to Southampton Gordon. Do you think you are the right man for the job?" It was akin to passing the ball across the face of his own goal – and Strachan pounced: "No. I think they should have got George Graham because I'm useless." It set the tone for his two and a half years on the south coast where asking the obvious was swiftly and savagely punished.

Reporter: "Gordon, you must be delighted with that result?"
Strachan: "You're spot-on! You can read me like a book."

Reporter: "This might sound like a daft question, but you'll be happy to get your first win under your belt, won't you?"
Strachan: "You're right. It is a daft question. I'm not even going to bother answering that one. It is a daft question, you're spot-on there."

Reporter: "You don't take losing lightly, do you Gordon?"
Strachan: "I don't take stupid comments lightly either."

He did make better journalists of those who dealt with him regularly – and those who kept themselves out of the firing line could enjoy the entertainment value he offered. His quick wit is still remembered with huge affection by all those who were not on the receiving end. They still recall seeing one journalist ask: "Gordon, can I have a quick word?" Instantly, he replied: "Velocity" – and walked off leaving one stunned reporter and a grinning crowd. And there were further classics, such as

Reporter: "So, Gordon, in what area do you think Middlesbrough were better than you today?"
Strachan: "Mainly that big green one out there..."

Reporter: *"There goes your unbeaten run. Can you take it?"*
Strachan: *"No, I'm just going to crumble like a wreck. I'll go home, become an alcoholic and maybe jump off a bridge."*

Reporter: *"Well done Gordon, you're fourth in the table – a Champions League spot. How will you celebrate tonight?"*
Strachan: *"I'm going to go home, put the league table on Teletext and watch that all night!"*

Even his own players did not escape. Claus Lundekvam's penalty for failing to score in some 300 league games was to hear his manager say on television that he should be booked for time-wasting every time he went up for a corner! But perhaps his best barb was reserved for Agustin Delgado who had Strachan pulling out his red hair in frustration. On one of the many days when the talented but troublesome Ecuadorian striker had failed to turn up for training, the manager was too exasperated to answer the inevitable question about the player's whereabouts. He said simply: "I've got more important things to think about. I've got a yoghurt on its sell-by date. I need to finish it today and that is far more important than worrying about Agustin Delgado."

LEGENDS LINE UP

In May 2008, an England Legends side beat a Scotland Legends team 2-0 at St Mary's in the Alan Ball Memorial Cup – with both sides managed by former Saints. Peter Reid took charge of England while Graeme Souness managed the Scots, who were beaten by first-half goals from Steve Hodge and Stan Collymore. Other former Saints playing in the match included Graeme Le Saux, Mark Wright, Chris Woods, David Speedie, Kerry Dixon and Mark Walters. Matthew Le Tissier – a player who flourished under Ball's management at Southampton – was unavailable because he was getting married. Former Saints hero Kevin Keegan presented the trophy to Alan Ball's son Jimmy who played the last 10 minutes in a fitting tribute to his father. A crowd of just over 13,500 turned out to pay tribute to the former Southampton midfielder and manager who had died from a heart attack just over a year earlier.

SPOT-ON

Saints went almost a decade without missing a penalty in open play. Jim Magilton saw his penalty saved against West Ham in April 1997 but – penalty shoot-outs apart – it was the last time Saints failed to score a spot-kick during a game until Nigel Quashie hit a post at QPR in January 2006.

LIVERPOOL FEEL PAINE

Terry Paine scored twice to give Saints a shock 2-1 win at Anfield in a League Cup third round tie in November 1960. The result clearly had a major impact on Bill Shankly's side who then opted out of the competition and refused to enter it for the next seven years.

CHINA SYNDROME

Mark Blake found himself involved in one of football's most bizarre transfers in February 2000 when he took the advice of former Saints striker Paul Rideout and joined Chinese side Chongging Vanguard. They were offering massive wages and it seemed almost too good to be true. It was. He settled in well and played three good games and was preparing for his fourth when a club official suddenly burst into his hotel room as the centre-back was sorting out his kit. The official spread his arms and began making noises like a plane. He then grabbed Blake's case, filled it with his clothes and bundled the bemused defender into a car. Blake found himself at Pusan airport where he was pushed through various checkpoints with no idea of what was going on. He was then abandoned and left to wait 48 hours before he could catch a plane to France, eventually arriving back England some £2,000 out of pocket. Not surprisingly he sought out Rideout and discovered that the Chinese club had unexpectedly lost their major sponsor leaving them potless!

FADE TO BLACK

Saints changed the colour of their home shorts from navy blue to the current colour of black during the 1949-50 season.

"SAINTS" LOSE 7-2

There was a bizarre case of mistaken identity when the London Saints Supporters Club went on tour to Prague in 1992. They arranged to play the local side in a friendly but were stunned to discover their hosts mistakenly believed they were playing the full Southampton side! Club stalwart Peter Berkeley recalls: "Communication then was not what it is now and we turned up to the town of Bezdekov and immediately began to worry when we saw posters advertising the game on every lamp post - it didn't help that we were suffering from the previous night's excesses! "It turned out that the game was in honour of the 80th anniversary of the town's football club - so it is fair to say we weren't quite what they were expecting! "We made our way to the changing room and having witnessed the 500 or so paying public, realised that we had a problem. Something else that took us by surprise was the pre-match formalities with each of their players presenting us with a bouquet of flowers followed by the playing of the national anthems (which our 'keeper cried through). "We found ourselves trailing 3-0 within 15 minutes but a combination of clearing hangovers and generous substituting by our hosts (taking off their better players) resulted in a 7-2 reverse - it could have been so much worse. The game had its lighter moments including our subs teaching the local kids to abuse our own keeper even though they didn't speak a word of English. "That evening we were guests of honour at a large celebratory banquet in the town hall. The language barrier was a problem so as a gesture of thanks we hijacked the brass band's instruments and played an unusual version of 'Oh when the Saints'!"

BROTHERLY LOVE

History was created when Ray Wallace received a call-up to the Saints side for their home game against Sheffield Wednesday in October 1988. He joined his twin Rodney and older brother Danny meaning Saints became the first club to field three brothers in a top-flight game since the 1919-20 season. Unfortunately the visitors spoiled the party with a 2-1 win at The Dell despite a Derek Statham penalty for a foul on Rod Wallace.

THE RUDDOCK STOMP

When Saints beat Aston Villa 3-1 at The Dell in November 1988, they went third in Division One, and embarked on a run of 17 league games without a win that saw them slide from the top three to the bottom three and seemingly certain relegation. Then, on April Fool's Day 1989 they faced bottom-three rivals Newcastle at The Dell in a classic six-pointer with both teams knowing the losers would almost certainly go down. It was a horribly tense and drab game with few chances of note. It had 0-0 written all over it until injury-time when Rod Wallace was brought down as he rounded the keeper. It was a reckless and needless challenge as the winger was heading away from goal but referee Gerald Ashby gloriously pointed to the spot. With so much at stake and confidence at an all-time low, few of the senior players fancied taking it in the absence of injured regular penalty-taker Derek Statham. And there was an audible groan as centre-back Neil Ruddock marched up and grabbed the ball in only his sixth game for the club. Many at the Milton Road End freely admit to ducking in anticipation of the ball soaring over the bar but the rugged defender held his nerve and buried the kick. It proved a turning point for Chris Nicholl's men who lost only one of their last eight games to finish a creditable 13th and six points clear of the drop zone. Newcastle went down!

PENALTY PAIN

Saints' golden touch from the spot deserted them in what was the biggest penalty shoot-out in the club's history as they chased a £50m prize in the 2007 play-offs. After scraping into sixth place, they faced Derby for a place at the newly rebuilt Wembley Stadium and a shot at the Premiership promised land. It finished 4-4 on aggregate and if away goals had counted double then Saints would have won through to the final. Instead it went to penalties at Pride Park. George Burley's side were immediately under pressure as the exhausted Leon Best fired wide of the right post. Andrew Surman, Rudi Skacel and Grzegorz Rasiak all found the net – but so too did the home side with unerring regularity. It meant Inigo Idiakez had to score his side's fifth and final spot-kick to give them a chance – but against his old club, the Spaniard fired high over the bar and Derby went on to Wembley and the Premiership.

NEIL RUDDOCK

STUNG BY HORNETS

Early in the 1980-81 season, Saints found themselves on the wrong end of one of the most remarkable come-backs in the history of the League Cup. With the newly-signed superstar Kevin Keegan in their side, Southampton ran up a seemingly decisive 4-0 win against Watford in the first leg of the second round tie at The Dell with two goals apiece from Charlie George and Nick Holmes. Lawrie McMenemy's men were to finish sixth in Division One where they were the second highest scorers with 76 goals while Graham Taylor's emerging Watford side were still two years away from promotion from Division Two. So the return leg surely had to be a formality… especially as it was well before the days of squad rotation and fielding weakened sides in cup competitions. Saints went to Vicarage Road without the injured Keegan but with an otherwise full-strength line-up for what looked likely to be merely a case of finishing off the job. But on an astonishing and unforgettable night the underdogs somehow turned it around. The Hornets gave themselves a glimmer of hope with a goal after 10 minutes and then a second on 35 minutes. It became "squeaky bum time" when the third went in on 67 minutes but the nerves should have been properly settled when a Sims own goal made it 5-3 on aggregate. But within a minute the home side had scored a penalty and reduced the arrears to just one goal once more. And with four minutes remaining, they levelled the tie overall. With away goals not counting double, it went to extra-time – and within a minute Watford had made it 6-1 on the night and 6-5 overall. Astonishingly they got a seventh six minutes from time to seal an incredible turn-around.

SAINTS' FIRST BLACK PLAYER

The first black footballer to play for Southampton was Alfred Pious Charles, a Trinidadian who made one appearance as an inside forward in the Second Division in 1937. It was more than 40 years before Tony Sealy became the club's second black player in 1979. He then appeared as a substitute in the 1979 League Cup final. Since then Saints have had a succession of black players, either home-grown or imported. In recent years the club have developed a hugely successful Racism Just Ain't Saintly campaign to stamp out racial prejudice.

INTERNATIONAL RESCUE

When George Burley became Scotland boss in January 2008, he completed a full house for Saints who have now seen one of their own go on to manage each of the home nations. Sir Alf was plain Alf Ramsey when he played as a full-back for Southampton from 1946 to 1949 before his move to Tottenham for the princely sum of £21,000. Moving into management in 1955, he led unfashionable Ipswich from Division Three (South) to the First Division title – an achievement which earned him the England job – and then World Cup glory in 1966. Two other Saints also went on to manage England. Kevin Keegan enjoyed less success on the international stage. As European Footballer of the Year, he stunned the football world by signing for Southampton in 1980 and was a huge crowd favourite before his departure to Newcastle. He took charge of England in February 1999 and resigned in October the following year. Bobby Robson played for Saints as an amateur in 1949 but did not make a first-team appearance. He went on to play for Fulham and West Brom before carving out a distinguished managerial career with Fulham, Ipswich and then England from 1982 until 1990. Lawrie McMenemy was assistant manager to Graham Taylor with England, taking charge of the under-21 side. He took the reins of Northern Ireland from 1998 until 1999 steadying the ship at a difficult time. Lawrie Sanchez signed associate schoolboy forms with Southampton in December 1974 and went on to manage Northern Ireland from 2004 to 2007. Mark Hughes played for Saints and managed Wales in tandem in 1999 before moving to Everton as he did not fit into the plans of new Southampton boss Glenn Hoddle. He then switched to Blackburn and featured in their Worthington Cup Final victory over Hoddle's Tottenham side. He later became Rovers manager, carving out a strong reputation. One other Saints player who went on to manage a national side was defender Tony Knapp. After signing from Leicester for £25,000 in 1961, he was ever-present as Saints reached the FA Cup semi-final in 1963. A commanding centre-back, he skippered Southampton's 1965-66 promotion success before joining Coventry in 1967. He played for Los Angeles, Wolves, Bristol City, Tranmere and Poole Town before carving out a successful managerial career taking charge of the Iceland national team, as well several Norwegian clubs.

WHERE WERE YOU WHEN FRANNY SCORED?

Claus Lundekvam's goalscoring record was surpassed by home-town hero Francis Benali who managed just one goal in 389 appearances. It came in December 1997 in a 2-1 win over Leicester at The Dell – and it surprised even Benali who had almost given up hope of ever finding the net for the team he had always supported. Matthew Le Tissier chipped in a long-range free-kick to pick out Benali just inside the penalty area. He had been left unmarked – probably because he was not regarded as a threat! Yet it is a mystery why he did not score more goals judging by the quality of the thumping header steered with power and precision into the top right corner. There was a second of silent disbelief as the magnitude of the moment sank in and then The Dell erupted in a deafening roar from fans who knew in an instant they had witnessed a special moment they would remember for ever. Benali's only other "goal" for the club came in his own testimonial in May 1997. The capacity crowd fully expected a diplomatic penalty to be awarded so that the popular defender could finally end his drought. Yet there was no need for such charity. Benali scored a genuine goal with an unlikely right-foot shot curled into the top right corner from 25 yards! His lack of goals for the club was all the more surprising as Benali began his career as a striker, playing up front for England Schoolboys at Wembley. Then a big, strapping forward who towered over his team-mates, Benali found his contemporaries catching up and overtaking him in height and he gradually made his way back through the team: first into midfield and then settling at left-back. Although not the most cultured on the ball, Benali wore his heart on his sleeve and was hugely popular with the fans who loved the fact he was one of their own. They also appreciated his total commitment and passion for the shirt. His driving will-to-win sometimes landed him in hot water with nine red cards in his career, usually for "red mist" offences. Off the field, he is the most polite, helpful and articulate man you could wish to meet. Over the years a succession of players were brought in with the intention of displacing him – but he saw them all off until finally the emergence of Wayne Bridge cost him his place. That prompted him to pull on a different shirt for the first time in his career with a successful loan spell at Nottingham Forest. However, his heart remained firmly at Southampton and he was happy to stay on and lend his experience to the young reserves and even played a part in the run to the 2003 FA Cup Final with a vital goal line clearance against Millwall in the fourth round. There was not a dry eye in the house when he made his final appearance in a Saints shirt with a cameo role in a mid-season friendly against Bayern Munich in January 2004. By then Benali was employed more in a coaching capacity but Gordon Strachan showed there is still room for sentiment by sending on Benali as a late substitute to an emotional ovation.

SAINTA CLAUS

In September 1996, Graeme Souness spent £350,000 to sign an unknown centre-back by the name of Claus Lundekvam from Norwegian side Brann Bergen. He was to stay with the club for 12 years, earning a richly-deserved testimonial against Celtic in July 2008. His classy calm on the ball earned him the nickname 'Silky' – a name which this keen sailor bestowed upon his yacht. As club captain, he became a popular figure with the fans – achieving cult hero status as much for his lack of goalscoring prowess as for his efficient defending. Indeed, manager Gordon Strachan famously quipped that Lundekvam should be booked for time-wasting whenever he went up for a corner because there was so little chance of him finding the net! However, that changed on April 3, 2004 when Saints won 4-1 at Wolves – and Lundekvam popped up unexpectedly in front of goal to turn in a free-kick by Fabrice Fernandes and beat his former team-mate Paul Jones. It was his first goal in 296 appearances for the club and it stunned the travelling supporters who were left wondering if it was some kind of belated April Fool's stunt. By a strange quirk, managing Wolves at the time was Lundekvam's former Southampton boss Dave Jones – and the Norwegian rubbed salt in the wounds by scoring his second – and last – league goal against Cardiff, also managed by Jones. Despite his lack of scoring form for Saints, remarkably Lundekvam did achieve the distinction of netting Norway's 1000th international goal.

ROYAL REWARD

The last time the Queen handed over the FA Cup was to Saints skipper Peter Rodrigues after the 1-0 win over Manchester United in 1976.

IN AT THE DEEP END

Saints were forced to hand a baptism of fire to 17-year-old apprentice Keith Granger in the final two games of the 1985-86 season. With Peter Shilton and his deputy Phil Kite both unavailable, manager Chris Nicholl had to turn to the raw youth team keeper for daunting fixtures at Everton and Tottenham. It was a big ask for the youngster who had a young and inexperienced defence in front of him and conceded 11 goals in those two games as he became the first Southampton schoolboy to rise through the ranks to the senior side since Bob Charles in 1959. Everton were pushing Liverpool all the way for the title and went into their penultimate game trailing their local rivals by an inferior goal difference of 12. For a while it looked as though they might wipe that out as they raced into a 4-0 lead by half-time. David Puckett got a consolation as Saints went down 6-1 at Goodison Park, following it up just two days later with a 5-3 defeat at White Hart Lane. Granger signed professional forms when he turned 18 in October that year but he was never given another first-team outing by Saints and moved to Darlington little over a year later. There he suffered a serious knee injury which required six operations and he eventually left when his contract expired in May 1990, returning to Hampshire to play for Basingstoke – who loaned him back to Saints to play for the reserves during another goalkeeping injury crisis. He maintained strong links with his home-town club, joining the coaching staff to work with the Academy goalkeepers in 2005.

SPOONFUL OF MADDISON HELPS SUGAR GO DOWN!

Saints midfielder Neil Maddison celebrated becoming a father just hours earlier by heading the only goal against Alan Sugar's Tottenham side at The Dell in November 1993.

TOP TURN-OUT

The biggest crowd Saints have played a league game in front of was the 70,302 who turned out to watch their 4-0 defeat at Tottenham in February 1950. That figure was beaten by the 100,000 who saw the 1976 FA Cup Final win against Manchester United.

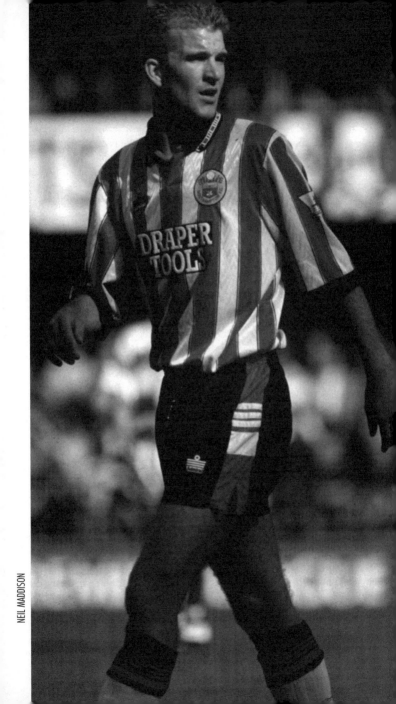

NEIL MADDISON

TOP OF THE LEAGUE

January 30, 1982 was a red letter day for Saints who went top of the old First Division for the first time in their history with a 1-0 win at Middlesbrough. Kevin Keegan got the all-important goal after just eight minutes, slotting in Alan Ball's slide-rule pass from a narrow angle. Manager Lawrie McMenemy said: "It is like winning the FA Cup all over again. To be top of the entire league in January is no mean feat." The victory saw Southampton leapfrog Manchester United to look down on 91 other clubs.

	P	W	D	L	F	A	Pts
SAINTS	22	12	4	6	40	30	40
Manchester United	22	11	6	5	33	18	39
Ipswich Town	19	12	2	5	36	28	38

McMenemy's men led the table for longer than any other side that season, remaining in front until March 20. Sadly Saints did not quite have the depth of squad to sustain the challenge and they could only finish seventh. A long-term injury to the free-scoring Steve Moran ruled him out of the second half of the season. He had netted nine in 18 games but then missed the last 22 fixtures of the campaign. Saints did still qualify for the UEFA Cup for a second successive season but fans were left with the thought of what might have been...

KEEPING FIT

Antti Niemi made history at the Millennium Stadium in 2003 for all the wrong reasons when he became the first goalkeeper ever to be carried off in an FA Cup final. The Finnish favourite suffered a bizarre calf injury midway through the second half of the 1-0 defeat by Arsenal. As he took a goal-kick he suddenly crumpled to the ground in obvious distress and lay prone in pain while Gunners fans whistled for the game to be stopped as Saints attacked at the other end, oblivious to their keeper's plight. He was replaced by Welsh keeper Paul Jones who took over in his country's home stadium and had the unique distinction of keeping a clean sheet in the FA Cup Final but finishing on the losing side at 90 minutes!

EXTRA WAIT

The Football League season was halted for a total of seven seasons because of the Second World War so Saints were itching to get going when Division Two resumed in August 1946. But they had to wait longer than their rivals as the eagerly-awaited resumption was delayed when their opening fixture against Newport County was called off because of a waterlogged pitch. Southampton – fielding eight debutants – eventually got under way on September 4 with a resounding 4-0 win at home to Swansea with a hat-trick from Doug McGibbon and a goal from Bob Veck.

VILLANS OF THE PIECE

Three times in "Great Escape" years, Saints pulled off fine wins in their penultimate game and came off the field expecting to be safe – only to find that Aston Villa had let them down. In 1995 they won 1-0 at Bolton which should have been enough – but Man City won at Villa Park. Two years later Saints beat Blackburn 2-0 at The Dell but found Villa had lost to Middlesbrough. And, in 1999 Southampton won 2-0 at Wimbledon and then discovered Charlton had got a last-minute winner at ten-man Villa. Saints could be forgiven for wondering if the Midlands side held a grudge against them as they needed only a point to ensure survival from their final game of the season at Villa Park in 1997. The Clarets also needed a draw to get into Europe but won 1-0 with an own goal by Richard Dryden. However other results ensured Southampton survived.

HERO AND VILLAN

Former Saints defender and manager Chris Nicholl achieved a unique distinction during his time with Aston Villa scoring all four goals in a 2-2 draw with Leicester City – a feat which has never been repeated.

ONE-OFF ACHIEVEMENT

Danny Wallace scored on his full England debut against Egypt in 1986 – but never played for his country again!

OLD TRAFFORD GLORY

Saints were involved in the first ever penalty shoot-out between two top-flight teams in the FA Cup when they beat Manchester United on their own ground. Second replays had been scrapped in a bid to cut fixture congestion and Ian Branfoot's side found themselves in a sudden-death decider in the fourth round in February 1992. After a goalless draw at The Dell, they went to Old Trafford for an unforgettable televised replay. Stuart Gray gave Southampton an eighth-minute lead, with his only goal for the club and Alan Shearer doubled the advantage. Andrei Kanchelskis pulled one back just before the break but Ian Branfoot's team battled for all they were worth and looked set to snatch a shock, but deserved, victory until the dying seconds. A clearance looked destined for a corner but hit Jeff Kenna and ricocheted across the face of goal to give Brian McClair a simple but hugely fortunate tap-in with no time left even to kick off! It looked to be game up for Saints, who were playing their third match in eight days and were expected to fold in extra-time. However, they stood strong through the additional 30 minutes – although they needed one slice of good fortune when Tim Flowers scrambled away a Bryan Robson header which looked to have crossed the line. So it went to penalties – at the Stretford End. Saints kept penalty king Matthew Le Tissier back for the expected crucial fifth spot-kick, but did not need him. Neil Ruddock, Alan Shearer, Micky Adams and Barry Horne all found the net while Neil Webb and a rookie Ryan Giggs both failed. Webb blasted high and wide to leave his side under pressure. Experienced campaigners Paul Ince and Bryan Robson did not shoulder the responsibility so it was left to Giggs whose effort was spectacularly saved by Flowers to his left, sparking memorable scenes. The keeper sprinted the length of the field to celebrate in front of the travelling supporters. He was chased all the way by Glenn Cockerill who was still carrying a cup of tea – and never spilled a drop!

LEEDS LOCK-OUT

Matthew Le Tissier scored against every side in the Premiership – apart from Leeds, much to the delight of his brother Carl who is a lifelong Leeds fan!

HOWELLS OF PROTEST

David Howells had a debut to remember as Saints visited newly-promoted Charlton for the second game of the season in August 1998. He came off the bench to bolster the midfield and finished the game in goal! Paul Jones was sent off for bringing down Clive Mendonca on 64 minutes – just seconds after manager Dave Jones had used his final substitute. Unable to bring on a keeper, Saints had to put an outfield player in goal – and Howells volunteered to the disappointment of the away fans who had hoped to see Matthew Le Tissier pull on the gloves. Traditionally, Le Tissier was always viewed as the "luxury" player to make way whenever Saints went down to 10 men – and he had shown outstanding goalkeeping skills in Francis Benali's testimonial. Even allowing for the non-competitive element of the game, he made a series of stunning saves and supporters were keen to see him try his hand in the heat of battle. However, Howells got there first and pulled rank. His first action was to face the resulting penalty scored by Mendonca who then netted twice more to complete a 5-0 rout.

AMBI-DEXTER-OUS

Saints suffered another bizarre goalkeeping injury in the fifth round of the competition in 2006. They were trailing 1-0 in a televised fifth round clash at Newcastle when Bartosz Bialkowski jumped unchallenged for a simple catch. He missed it and landed awkwardly, crumpling to the ground and instantly signalling he was hurt. Home fans jeered thinking he was putting it on to cover up for his error but the Polish under-21 international had badly damaged cruciate ligaments. He needed a reconstruction which put him out of action for almost a year. Saints had already used their three substitutes so striker Dexter Blackstock volunteered to take over between the sticks – despite never having played there in his life. He gave a hugely entertaining if somewhat comical display, almost playing "rush keeper". He almost conceded direct from a corner when he wandered off his line but recovered his ground just in time to scoop clear. But his presence in goal left the 10 men with no attacking threat and they went down 1-0.

MCGIBBON MAGIC

Doug McGibbon scored six goals as Saints hammered Chelsea 7-0 in December 1945. The League programme was still on hold after the Second World War so Saints continued to play in League South in readiness for the resumption of Division Two fixtures the following year. McGibbon scored twice in a 3-2 win over Tottenham on December 15, then once in the 4-3 defeat by the same opposition a week later. It was an intensive festive programme and he netted again in a 4-1 win over Brentford on Christmas Day and again in the return fixture on Boxing Day as Saints went down 4-3. On December 29 Saints were playing their fourth game in eight days but showed no signs of fatigue as they hammered Chelsea with McGibbon getting a personal best six goals, including one just five seconds after kick-off at the start of the second half. Timing then was not as exact as it is now so estimates varied though five seconds became the generally accepted time, setting a new league record.

STUNNING NEWS

It is rare to pull off a transfer coup which has not leaked out to the media but Saints shook the football world in February 1980 when Lawrie McMenemy mysteriously called a press conference at the Potters Heron near Romsey. The assembled journalists had no clue why they had been summoned and were baffled as the manager spoke in vague terms about plans for the future – until he received the signal that his "special guest" had arrived. McMenemy said: "And now I'd like you to meet a man who is going to play a big part in the future of Southampton Football Club..." Hardened hacks, who thought they had seen it all, were stunned into silence – and then applause – as Kevin Keegan walked in! The current European Footballer of the Year had agreed to leave Hamburg and sign for Southampton. The seeds for the audacious coup were sown when McMenemy rang his friend Keegan and asked him to bring over some light fittings from Germany on his next trip home. By the end of the conversation Keegan had been persuaded to become a Saint for a fee of just £400,000. There was just one snag – he forgot to bring the light fittings!

GIVE IT TO RON

The fans' chant of "Give it to Ron!" took on a poignant new meaning 40 years on. Ron Davies' haul of 43 goals in his 1966-67 debut season for Saints will surely never be beaten and the memory still burns bright with all those fortunate enough to have witnessed his phenomenal contribution in the club's first ever top-flight campaign. Many came from the head of the Welsh wizard sparking the crowd's cry which developed a very different objective in 2007. "Give it to Ron" became the slogan for an appeal to raise money for The Dell legend to have a badly-needed hip replacement following years of suffering caused by the repetitive strain of his trademark salmon-like leap. Davies hails from an era when footballers played solely for the love of the game and not for the vast millions which are now thrust upon very ordinary players who could not have held a candle to him in his prime. Without that financial security behind him, Davies had to put up with the pain in his New Mexico trailer park home and when his plight came to light, Saints fans were typically quick to rally round and offer to help - a gesture which moved the proud Welshman to tears. The pain was in his left hip which was the leg he used to take off with and without surgery, he would have been left in a wheelchair and unable to work. For those too young to remember this footballing genius, Ron Davies was once described by no lesser light than Sir Matt Busby as the "best centre-forward in Europe". That was in August 1969 after Davies had netted all four goals for Saints in a sensational 4-1 win at a star-studded Manchester United team which included Bobby Charlton, Denis Law and George Best. Busby repeatedly tried to sign the Welsh international but to their eternal credit Saints refused to sell - and in those days there was no freedom of contract. Southampton got the best out of him before selling him to Pompey. By the time United landed their man he was past his best and he made just eight appearances for them before moving to America. The club's record signing at £55,000 from Norwich, Ron the Nod scored a phenomenal 134 goals in 239 league appearances, many of them with his head. He finished his inaugural season with Southampton with the stunning tally of 43 goals, including 37 in the league. He fed off the meat-and-drink crosses supplied by the wing wizards of Terry Paine and John Sydenham forging a strong partnership with Martin Chivers, and with Mike Channon, who described him as the best header of a ball he had ever seen. Davies had a colossal leap which often saw his head higher than the crossbar and he also had an uncanny knack of hanging in the air to meet the ball with power and precision. His secret was the training he did at his first club Chester when manager Bill Lambton made him wear heavy army boots to run and to jump hurdles. Davies laughed: "They weighed several kilos and when I took them off and put football boots on, I felt I could jump 20 feet. It helped build up the strength in my legs but there was also a psychological effect. I had no idea how good I was in the air until Southampton signed me from Norwich. The funny thing was I had never really played that well against them but Ted Bates obviously saw something special in me because he paid a club record fee. He was a great manager and the nicest guy you could wish to meet. I loved him to bits. The way he treated players was fantastic. He was Southampton Football Club. And the system he used was just perfect for me and the way I played the game. With Terry Paine and John Sydenham slinging the crosses in, it was just right for me and the way I played the game. It had always been my dream to play in the top division and Ted gave me that chance. It was such a thrill and I finished that first season as the top scorer in Britain with 43 goals. The next season was harder as people knew all about me and I was double-marked the whole time. I used to joke I'd go to the toilet at half-time and come and find a defender waiting for me!" In addition to his phenomenal goal-scoring record, Davies also made a name for himself as a talented artist, caricaturing his team-mates in the Echo. Even now, he still keeps his hand in and drew Matthew Le Tissier, auctioning off the print to raise money for the appeal.

CHOCOLATE BOXES

The Chocolate Boxes was the nickname affectionately afforded to a unique section of terracing at The Dell. With no room for expansion out onto Milton Road, the club constructed three raised platforms at the back of the terrace in 1949. Split into three sections these quirky structures became a distinctive part of the ground's homely character until they were demolished in 1981.

GLOBAL A-Z

From Australia to Zimbabwe, Saints have fielded internationals from all over the world. Southampton players have represented a total of 23 different countries during their time with the club. Until the global expansion of the game in the 1990s, international players traditionally hailed from one of the five countries in the British Isles. However Saints became trail-blazers in bringing in top foreign imports when Lawrie McMenemy signed Yugoslav defender Ivan Golac in 1978. Although he never actually represented his country while at The Dell, he is widely recognised as the first "foreigner" to play in a Wembley final, appearing in the 3-2 League Cup defeat by Nottingham Forest. Saints also broke new ground by signing Russian duo Alexei Cherednik and Sergei Gotsmanov, who had memorably scored in a 2-0 win against England at Wembley in 1984. However, the language barrier proved impossible for them to overcome and neither produced their best form while at The Dell, costing them their international places too. The club's post-war internationals are:

Australia	Robbie Slater
Belgium	Jelle Van Damme
Canada	Jim Brennan
Cape Verde Islands	Pele
Colombia	Jhon Viafara
Democratic Republic of Congo	Cedric Baseya
Ecuador	Agustin Delgado. Kleber Chala
England	Bill Ellerington, Alf Ramsey
	Terry Paine , Mike Channon
	Dave Watson, David Armstrong
	Kevin Keegan, Peter Shilton
	Steve Williams, Danny Wallace
	Mark Wright, Alan Shearer
	Tim Flowers, Matthew Le Tissier
	Wayne Bridge, James Beattie, Peter Crouch
Finland	Antti Niemi
Ireland	Fred Kiernan, Tommy Traynor
	Tony Byrne, Austin Hayes
	Alan McLoughlin, Rory Delap

Jamaica ....Ricardo Fuller
Latvia............................Marian Pahars, Imants Bleidelis
Morocco ....Youssef Safri
....................................Hassan Kachloul, Tahar El Khalej
Northern Ireland .... Hugh Kelly, Jimmy Shields
.... Chris Nicholl, Colin Clarke
....Jim Magilton, Iain Dowie, Chris Baird
Norway...Claus Lundekvam
.... Egil Ostenstad, Jo Tessem
Poland... Grzegorz Rasiak
....................................Marek Saganowski, Kamil Kosowski
Scotland...Ian Black, Neil McCann
....Stephen Crainey, Nigel Quashie
Senegal .... Henri Camara
Sweden .... Anders Svensson, Michael Svensson
.... Mikael Nilsson, Alexander Ostlund
Trinidad and Tobago ....Kenwyne Jones, Stern John
Tunisia..Alaeddine Yahia
Wales.. Gareth Bale, Mark Hughes
.... Paul Jones, Barry Horne
.... Stuart Williams, Ron Davies
.... Alan Neilson, Alan Curtis
Zimbabwe.. Bruce Grobbelaar

DEREK'S DECIDER

Perhaps the most remarkable game ever at The Dell was in December 1960 when Saints hosted Leeds in the fourth round of the League Cup. It did not start well with the floodlights failing before kick-off to cause a 29-minute delay. Derek Reeves put the home side in front with a header but they suffered a set-back five minutes later when goalkeeper Ron Reynolds was carried off. At that point the lights failed again and when they came back on, defender Cliff Huxford was in goal, as substitutes had yet to be invented. Reeves scored three more to put the 10 men 4-0 up and in a seemingly unassailable position. But astonishingly fellow Second Division side Leeds hit four goals of their own to draw level. With just 30 seconds remaining, Saints grabbed a winner; inevitably Reeves was the scorer to finish with all five of his side's goals.

DYER MISFORTUNE

Matthew Le Tissier was lined up for an emotional farewell as he prepared to hang up his boots in May 2002. Persistent injury problems had sidelined him for much of the season and he was still not match-fit when Newcastle visited St Mary's for the final game of the campaign. However, with his side safe from the possibility of relegation, manager Gordon Strachan sprang a surprise by naming the crowd favourite on the bench. The intention was to bring him on 10 minutes from time for a well-deserved ovation and the chance to say an emotional farewell – maybe even to score one last goal. But those plans were scuppered when Saints were reduced to 10 men 10 minutes after half-time. As Kieron Dyer went haring down the right wing, he was brutally taken out by Tahar El Khalej who launched himself into a sliding tackle from a long distance out. The resulting injury cast a huge doubt over Dyer's involvement in that summer's World Cup and saw the Moroccan defender instantly red-carded. It also spelled the end of Le Tissier's dreams of a dramatic swansong. Strachan had shown there is still room for sentiment in the game by including the long-serving star among the substitutes, but with prize money of around £500,000 a place, he also had to bear in mind the cold, harsh financial implications. At the time Saints were leading 2-1 and desperately hanging on with 10 men – and the manager felt he could not justify bringing on an unfit luxury player, purely out of goodwill. He brought on three more defensively-minded replacements – and his decision was justified as Saints held out to win the game and climb three places in the table. A draw would have cost the club £1.5m in prize money and a defeat would have left them £2m poorer. The ultimate irony, for those hoping for a repeat of Le Tissier's last goal at The Dell, was that Saints did get a third goal in the final minute. And it was a trademark Le Tissier strike, lobbed over Shay Given from 35 yards – but by the unlikely figure of Paul Telfer rather than the man affectionately known as Le God.

WHAT'S IN A NAME

Saints favourite Danny Wallace's real name is actually David Lloyd Wallace – Danny was a nickname. And, Kevin Keegan's first name is Joseph. Kevin is his middle name.

ROD, DANNY AND RAY WALLACE

ENGLAND EXPECTS

In 1982 Saints fielded six past or future England captains. Mick Channon, Dave Watson, Peter Shilton, Kevin Keegan, Mick Mills and Alan Ball all played for Southampton during that calendar year, though never in the same team.

NAZI SURPRISE

The docks made Southampton a prime target for German bombers during the Second World War. The Dell suffered several hits including the West Stand. However the worst damage was caused in November 1940 by a bomb which landed in the Milton Road end of the ground, leaving an 18-foot crater. It caused a culvert to burst and flood the pitch leaving it unplayable. That meant Saints had to look for other grounds to play their games and even ended up playing a "home" Cup match against Brentford at Fratton Park. Saints played the last two thirds of their campaign away from home and finished third from bottom in the Southern Regional League. That meant a succession of tedious journeys in pitch dark due to the war-time black-out. None was worse than the return trip from Cardiff which saw the team arrive back at noon on the Sunday following a night in the open after their coach first hit a wall, and then suffered a puncture, after getting lost in the dark.

WRETCHED REPEAT

That infamous 4-3 FA Cup defeat at Tranmere sparked a cruel joke. What kind of house do Saints fans live in? Three up, four down! And it gained a new lease of life when it happened again in November 2005 when Saints were at home to a struggling Leeds side in the Coca-Cola Championship. Two goals from Nigel Quashie and one from Marian Pahars seemed to have wrapped it up by half-time and with 19 minutes remaining, the home side were still comfortably cruising to a seemingly routine victory. Paul Butler got what looked to be a consolation on 71 minutes but the nerves were set jangling when Robbie Blake pulled another one back six minutes later. A David Healy penalty provided an unlikely equaliser and as Saints tried to hang on grimly, Kenny Miller nicked a winner four minutes from time.

THE EXORCIST

Saints failed to win any of their first five league games at St Mary's – plus their prestige pre-season friendly against Espanyol. That led to talk of a curse on the ground which was built on the old Anglo-Saxon settlement of Hamwic. On November 23, 2001 the *Southern Daily Echo* arranged for a local pagan priestess Cerradwen "Dragonoak" Connelly to perform an exorcism on the site. The following afternoon Saints beat Charlton 1-0 with a goal by Marian Pahars with a goalbound Athletic effort somehow bouncing back off the inside of the left post in the final minute.

FLOODING BACK

Saints fans staged a mass exodus as Bolton hit what looked a certain winner in an FA Cup fifth round replay at The Dell in February 1992. In the initial tie, Southampton had squandered a 2-0 lead in the televised first game at Wanderers' old Burnden Park ground as Richard Hall's brace was cancelled out during the second half. However Ian Branfoot's men were confident of beating the second-tier opponents at The Dell and took the lead through Alan Shearer, only for Walker to capitalise on a Tim Flowers error to level just before the break. Just as extra-time loomed, Darby smacked in a volley in the 90th minute to send the home supporters streaming for the exits. Injury-time was virtually up when Barry Horne picked up the ball just inside the visitors' half and strode forward. With no time to do anything else he chanced his luck with a shot from fully 35 yards – and the ball flew like a rocket into the top right corner of the Milton Road goal. The hundreds who had left early missed one of *the* great moments – and did a sudden about-turn. They crowded back into the ground for extra-time and saw Horne grab his second goal, although in much less spectacular fashion. He needed the help of a deflection, but it was enough to give Saints a 3-2 win. But for his thunderous equaliser, it would have been the first time since 1950 that Saints had drawn away to a team from a lower division and then lost the replay at home. On the previous occasion they had lost as a Second Division side, to Northampton in the league below.

NAMING THE DELL

The Dell got its name because of the babbling brook which ran through the middle of the pitch that had to be covered over before the ground was built in 1898. The spring had initially run through the Common but had been diverted in medieval times to serve the city. It continued to flow under the pitch until The Dell was demolished – occasionally causing problems with drainage. Although it was grossly inadequate for the Premier League when Southampton eventually moved in 2001, at the time it was the most up-to-date stadium in the country. That was down to the generosity of local fishmonger and ardent Saints fan George Thomas who ploughed £10,000 into buying and developing the site and who charged the club just £250 a year in rent until 1906 when the lease came up for renewal. The rent was set to double to £500 a year – a figure rejected by the board. Saints looked set to move home until the price was dropped to £400 a year and a deal was signed. Saints bought the freehold from his widow in 1926 and promptly built a new stand and enlarged an existing one instead of improving the team. They had become the first champions of the new Division Three (South) in 1921 and held their own comfortably at the higher level. Many fans wanted the board to invest in the team and push on to Division One but they put the cash into bricks and mortar. That strategy backfired spectacularly just after the end of the 1928-29 season when the older of the two stands was destroyed by fire. The club had to take on a further £10,000 of debt to rebuild it.

LIGHTS OUT

The final floodlit league game at The Dell was a gloomy 3-0 home defeat by Ipswich on April 2, 2001. It was live on Sky and Stuart Gray's first game as caretaker boss. His side were well beaten, conceding their first league goals since their 2-1 defeat at Liverpool on New Year's Day. They then embarked on a seven-match unbeaten run in the Premiership drawing 0-0 at home to Charlton, and at Tottenham, before winning five on the spin. They defeated Leicester 1-0, and Bradford 2-0, at The Dell, then won 1-0 at Middlesbrough and Man City before Hoddle signed off with a 1-0 victory at home to Everton.

OFF THE MARK

After drawing a blank in their opening home game at St Mary's – a 2-0 defeat by Chelsea – Saints scored their first league goal at St Mary's when Marian Pahars nodded in against Aston Villa. However, it was not enough to prevent a 3-1 defeat.

SPECTACULAR SLIP

Saints and their fans were left shell-shocked after seeing a 2-0 lead over-turned by Spurs at The Dell during an FA Cup fifth round replay in March 1995. A penalty scored by Matthew Le Tissier had earned a well-deserved 1-1 draw at White Hart Lane to set up a mouth-watering return. By half-time Saints were two up and cruising as an opportunist strike by Neil Shipperley, and another Le Tissier penalty put them seemingly in command and on their way to the quarter-finals. Tottenham boss Gerry Francis sent on Ronny Rosenthal, more in hope than expectation, as the former Liverpool striker had managed just one goal all season – and that was in a third round tie against non-league Altrincham. But the Israeli international scored twice to force extra-time. Suddenly the momentum was with the north London side. With 11 minutes of the extra-time period played, Rosenthal unleashed a 25-yard thunderbolt which left Bruce Grobbelaar wrong-footed to give the visitors a 3-2 lead. Saints gambled on attack and left gaps at the back – with fatal consequences. They were repeatedly hit on the break and further goals by Teddy Sheringham, Nicky Barmby and Southampton-born Darren Anderton gave the visitors an astonishing 6-2 win. They also became the first team ever to put six goals past Saints in the FA Cup, and it was the club's heaviest defeat in the competition since they had been thumped 5-0 at home to Manchester City in 1910.

RICHARDS RICHES

When Dean Richards made his acrimonious move to Tottenham in October 2001 they pocketed a new club record fee of £8.1m – not bad business on a player they picked up for nothing.

SAINTS GIVEN A LIFT

Four Coventry players found themselves trapped in a hotel lift before their game at The Dell in 1978. They were released by the fire brigade in time for the kick-off but must have wished they had stayed put as Saints won 4-0 with goals by Malcolm Waldron, Trevor Hebberd, Phil Boyer and Graham Baker.

RETURN VISIT

Tranmere Rovers were the last visitors to play a cup-tie at The Dell – and also the first at St Mary's. The Birkenhead side drew 0-0 in the fifth round of the FA Cup in 2001 and were then paired against Saints in the Worthington League Cup in September 2002. In between, Southampton had had three away ties in the League Cup and one away game in the FA Cup in 2001-02 so they had to wait a full year to stage their first cup-tie at their new ground. This time Tranmere were soundly beaten 6-1. Chris Marsden opened the scoring after just 16 seconds: Saints' quickest opener since Tommy Mulgrew against Brentford in 1954. Brett Ormerod grabbed a hat-trick, Southampton's first since Matthew Le Tissier against Nottingham Forest in the opening game of the 1995-96 season.

HOBSON'S CHOICE

When Gordon Hobson moved to Lincoln in September 1988, the Imps paid a club record fee of £60,000. He is best remembered for a hat-trick in a 4-2 win at Manchester City in April 1987. It made him the first Southampton player to score three on the road since Ron Davies memorably netted four at Old Trafford in 1969.

WAYNES' WINDMILL

Home-grown hero Wayne Bridge scored his first away goal for Saints in a 1-1 draw at Bolton in September 2002, bursting forward to hit a powerful left foot shot from just inside the area. He celebrated with a "windmill" arm-whirling as a tribute to his father's hero, Saints legend Mike Channon.

NIGHTMARE AT ELM PARK

Saints found themselves the victims of a hoax call as they prepared to take on Reading in the Coca-Cola League Cup in November 1995. After heavy rain, they received a phone call telling them the fourth round tie was off as the Elm Park pitch was flooded. The players were just about to board the coach in mid-afternoon but were sent home and told they had the evening off. Unfortunately, it was all false and the game was still on! When Saints discovered the truth, there was a frantic succession of calls to try and get the players back. In the days before mobile phones, it was not easy to track them all down and so they did not arrive at the Berkshire ground until little more than half an hour before kick-off. With little time to prepare themselves or to get themselves mentally focused, Saints were never in the game and went down 2-1 in the driving rain to the underdogs despite Ken Monkou heading an equaliser from a Matthew Le Tissier free-kick. Lee Nogan and Trevor Morley netted for the First Division team.

CUP DOUBLE

In the 1998-99 season, Saints were drawn against Fulham in both the League Cup and the FA Cup. As was usual in this era, Southampton were struggling for survival in the top division, while the West London club were upwardly mobile in the third tier following the arrival of Harrods owner and multi-millionaire Mohammed Al Fayed. Even so, on paper, it seemed a straightforward enough prospect over two legs in the second round of the Worthington League Cup, especially after a 1-1 draw at Craven Cottage: thanks to James Beattie's 20-yard toe-poke. But Saints lost the return 1-0 and to make matters worse, had Carlton Palmer sent off in the process. Later that season, Fulham proved it was no fluke when they were drawn at The Dell in the third round of the FA Cup. Managed by former Saints hero Kevin Keegan, the Cottagers led until the dying seconds when Egil Ostenstad swivelled on the ground and forced the ball home to give Saints unlikely salvation and force a replay at Craven Cottage. However, it all proved in vain as Fulham's Barry Hayles netted a winner for the underdogs just five minutes from the end of the replay.

TURNING JAPANESE

St Mary's hosted its first full international in September 2001 when 11,801 turned out to watch Japan and Nigeria fight out a 2-2 draw in torrential rain which left a corner of the pitch waterlogged and almost forced an abandonment.

NIGHTMARE AT ELM PARK 2

Having lost to Reading in dubious circumstances in the League Cup in 1995, Saints were given a swift chance to exact revenge as the FA Cup draw handed them a third round tie back at Elm Park. The country was in the grip of a big freeze and only three third round ties survived – although the decision to press ahead with the Reading game remained a contentious issue long after the final whistle. The fixture was in doubt almost until the kick-off with the pitch frozen and rock solid. Referee Graham Poll decided it was little different to playing on hard summer surfaces and is reported to have famously said it would be OK as long as the players only went at it 90 per cent! Saints boss Graeme Souness was deeply unhappy with the decision – and possibly his players might have been affected by the obvious unease at playing on an iron-hard surface. The visitors started well and seemed to have adapted to the conditions – and to their lack of support – with many fans declining to travel in the belief the game would be called off. But then Claus Lundekvam, making his first appearance in the competition, was caught in possession as he looked to pick out a pass rather than hoof it clear. The ball was whipped off his toe to set up Lambert for the opener on 19 minutes but just four minutes after half-time Saints levelled when Eyal Berkovic picked out Egil Ostenstad through the inside right channel. He held off three defenders to fire across the keeper and just inside the base of the far left post. Within six minutes Darren Caskey had volleyed the home side back in front and it got worse 13 minutes from time when Francis Benali was sent off for an elbow on Trevor Morley who scored the resulting penalty to make it 3-1. To round off a wretched afternoon, Robbie Slater made an abusive gesture to a linesman in the dying minutes and he too received a red card. Souness had to be restrained by stewards at the final whistle as he attempted to remonstrate with the referee.

JOHN CORBETT

To this day, Saints are still indebted to the foresight and generosity of John Corbett, one of the great gentlemen of the game. Very much part of the Old School, he was more than happy to dip his hand into his own pocket to help the club through troubled times rather than asking what was in it for him. He died aged 92 in January 1998 leaving the club a lasting legacy in terms of its values of honesty and decency – as well as a far more tangible asset. In 1969 he had the foresight to buy a 40-acre site of seemingly little commercial value out in the countryside. But the housing boom and the spread of Southampton and Eastleigh meant that it increased hugely in value. In 1989 Bovis Homes paid the club £500,000 for a 20-year option on the site allowing them to buy it for 90 per cent of the market value if planning permission were ever granted. With only a year of the agreement remaining – that still had not happened – Saints had received half a million for nothing, and still have the chance to sell the land for development if it is no longer classified as Green Belt. That could net them millions. Businessmen these days are as likely to look at the share price as the scores but that way of thinking was totally alien to John Corbett who never wanted his significant shareholding to be worth anything. He was elected onto the reconstituted board in 1936 when the club was on its uppers and struggling to survive in the depression. They had to borrow money from Norwich Union in order to keep going and John Corbett had to ask his uncle to pay the club's summer wage bill. For a time he was both acting manager and chairman – and loved the image of picking the team and then presenting it to himself in the boardroom! He had a passion for horses and bred the 1951 Grand National winner Nickel Coin and helped train the 1946 winner Lovely Cottage. He received an award from the FA as the longest-serving director in the country before becoming the club president. His family farmed 650 acres at Cheriton and thousands more on the Scottish island of Mull from where this remarkable man would travel for Southampton home games despite never owning a passport or flying in an aeroplane! In 2006 the Corbett name once again figured prominently when his daughter Mary was appointed as a director of the football club board. A lifelong Saints fan, she shared her father's selfless ideals as well as his passion for the club. She stepped down in May 2008.

PRICE IS RIGHT

Saints now have one of the most up-to-date training grounds in the country thanks to local businessman Peter Price. In 1982 he bought and built a small stadium in the village of Marchwood for his non-league side Road-Sea who had risen through the ranks of the Wessex League to gain admission to the Southern League. They almost made it to the Conference but crowds dwindled and Price began to lose interest in the club which folded in 1987 leaving the ground empty and unused. It was perfect for Saints who until then trained on the Southampton University playing fields at Eastleigh. They bought the prime land for a knock-down price – but with clauses in the contract that there would be a significant surcharge if it were ever given planning permission for commercial development or housing. At the time there was just one small stand and changing rooms by the main pitch with one small field for training. Saints began to develop it and added offices and a gym then a medical room and players' restaurant. They expanded territorially too buying adjoining fields and turning them into training pitches for the Academy teams. They also built an indoor training area and installed an outdoor artificial pitch to enable the players to keep working in bad weather. The shock appointment of Rugby World Cup winner Sir Clive Woodward in 2005 took the facilities to a new level. A keen believer in sports science, he expanded the indoor training dome adding more offices, a new weights room, a players' lounge and a "war room" equipped with computer screens for ProZone analysis of games. They were facilities befitting the Premier League just as the club dropped into the Coca-Cola Championship. Saints regularly play their home reserve games at the training ground, named Staplewood because it adjoins Staplewood Lane.

THE FISHER KING

Saints were just seconds from defeat in their FA Cup third round tie at home to Aston Villa in January 1976 when Hughie Fisher drilled a dramatic last-gasp equaliser to force a 1-1 draw. Lawrie McMenemy's men won the replay 2-1 and went on to Wembley winning the FA Cup for the only time in their history. There was no romantic reward for Fisher who was an unused substitute on the great day.

OOOH TERRY HURLOCK

As news leaked out of Terry Hurlock's impending £400,000 transfer from Glasgow Rangers to Southampton, television crews assembled in The Dell car park to capture his arrival. They filmed every posh car which pulled in but took no notice of a battered old brickies' van – until the rear doors opened and Hurlock clambered out wearing a Hawaiian shirt and wide grin. The low-key arrival was typical of a down-to-earth honest midfield battler who was more than just a hard-man destroyer. For some the long-haired enforcer came to symbolise manager Ian Branfoot's more robust approach. He could play a bit too and he quickly became a cult hero on the terraces.

SUBSTITUTES

It was not until 1965-66 that substitutes were allowed to be used – and then only when a player was hurt. However, this soon led to players feigning injury if the manager wanted to make a tactical switch. That rule lasted just two years. Ken Wimshurst was Saints' first substitute coming on in the home game against Coventry in September 1965 when goalkeeper John Hollowbread sustained a knee injury which ended his career. Cliff Huxford went in goal and kept a clean sheet as Saints won 1-0 with a Martin Chivers goal.

THIS IS A DODD-LE!

Jason Dodd must have thought playing in the top-flight was a doddle after winning his first two games 4-1. Signed from his home-town club of Bath City for a bargain £50,000, he made his debut at QPR on October 14, 1989. Rod Wallace netted twice with the other goals coming from Alan Shearer, and a Matthew Le Tissier penalty on his birthday. If that was a special start, it got even better the following week as Saints hosted mighty Liverpool and gave the undefeated League leaders a sound beating. It is no exaggeration to say Saints could have had six or seven as they also struck the woodwork twice on an unforgettable afternoon. However, they had to settle for two goals from Rod Wallace, one from Le Tissier and a header by Paul Rideout from a cross by Dodd, who marked the lethal John Barnes out of the game.

JASON DODD

GREAT ESCAPES PART ONE: 1993-94

Saints were marooned in 21st place with only doomed Swindon below them when Ian Branfoot was sacked in January 1994. That changed the mood among the fans and caretaker duo Lew Chatterley and Dave Merrington oversaw a 1-0 win at home to Coventry before the "Dream Ticket" partnership was unveiled. Alan Ball was appointed as manager with Lawrie McMenemy as Director of Football to spark a remarkable revival. Their first game in charge saw Saints stun Newcastle with a 2-1 win at St James' Park and their first Dell fixture produced a memorable 4-2 win over Liverpool in the snow live on Sky. Matthew Le Tissier hit a hat-trick which included two penalties and an opener after just 28 seconds. Craig Maskell got the other on his second debut for the club. Saints owed much to the stunning form of Le Tissier who had been inexplicably dropped by Branfoot in the autumn of 1993. The manager would claim that action inspired the mercurial magician to respond with some stunning goals including an unforgettable double at home to Newcastle on Sky. However, it was the decision of Ball and McMenemy to give him a free role which paid most dividends. They built the team around their star man instructing the others to get the ball to him at every opportunity – and Le Tissier responded with 15 goals in 16 games. The run included two hat-tricks and a sensational last-minute winner at home to Wimbledon when a free-kick was rolled to him, he flipped the ball up and volleyed into the top right corner from 25 yards. Despite the upturn in fortunes, Saints looked to be heading for the drop as they lost three consecutive "six-pointers" against relegation rivals Oldham, Chelsea and Manchester City over Easter. That left them second from bottom with just six games remaining, a sequence which was to include two more defeats. But a sensational 5-4 win at Norwich breathed new life into the season. It was followed by a 3-1 win at home to Blackburn who went on to finish runners-up. It went to the wire with five clubs still in with a chance of taking the final relegation place on the last day of the season. Saints had their fate in their own hands but faced a tricky fixture at West Ham, not helped by their late arrival because of heavy traffic. They started poorly going behind after just 11 minutes but then Le Tissier curled in a trademark free-kick for the equaliser just before the break. Le Tissier set up Neil Maddison for a header to put his side in front on 52 minutes only for the home side to equalise 10 minutes later. A Le Tissier penalty seemed to make Saints safe but they had to endure a nervy finale amid chaotic scenes. Upton Park was about to lose its terraces and their fans wanted to celebrate. They thought the final whistle had sounded and invaded the pitch only to be sent packing by the referee with two minutes still to play. Hundreds stood lining the pitch, not just within touching distance of the players but in some cases even impeding them. That was a significant factor in Ken Monkou turning the ball into his own net from close range, sparking a second pitch invasion. Thankfully it did not prove costly as results elsewhere meant Saints were safe by a point as the referee gave up the battle and blew the final whistle. Chelsea's injury-time winner at Stamford Bridge meant Sheffield United went down, the first time all afternoon they had dropped into the bottom three.

Premiership Table 1993-94

	P	W	D	L	F	A	Pts
Tottenham Hotspur	42	11	12	19	54	59	45
Manchester City	42	9	18	15	38	49	45
Everton	42	12	8	22	42	63	44
Southampton	42	12	7	23	49	66	43
Ipswich Town	42	9	16	17	35	58	43
Sheffield United	42	8	18	16	42	60	42
Oldham Athletic	42	9	13	20	42	68	40
Swindon Town	42	5	15	22	47	100	30

THE I'S HAVE IT

Inigo Idiakez is the only player ever to play in the league for the Saints with a surname beginning with the letter I. The Spanish midfielder joined from Derby in August 2006. He made his debut in a 2-1 defeat at Ipswich but suffered from a series of hamstring problems. He was loaned out to QPR to regain match fitness and returned for the end of season play-off semi-final at Derby where he missed the decisive penalty in a sudden-death shoot-out for a place at Wembley.

GREAT ESCAPES PART TWO: 1995-96

This was horribly tight as Saints went into their final game of the campaign at home to a Wimbledon side who were already safe, but renowned for fighting for every ball. Dave Merrington had had little cash to spend with the reduced capacity limiting his budget. Apart from buying promising keeper Neil Moss for £200,000, his only real outlay was £850,000 for experienced campaigner Barry Venison from Galatasaray. The legendary Spirit of Southampton shone through as they beat champions-elect Manchester United 3-1 in the infamous "grey shirt" game in April thanks to first-half goals by Ken Monkou, Neil Shipperley and Matthew Le Tissier. Saints thought they had secured survival in their penultimate match as they won 1-0 at Bolton who were relegated as a result. But they came off the pitch to discover rivals Coventry had won at Wimbledon while Manchester City had achieved a shock victory at fourth-placed Aston Villa. Southampton though were in the driving seat on the last day. Their superior goal difference meant they would survive if they won at home to the Dons. In a nutshell, they had to do the same or better than Man City at home to Liverpool or better than Coventry at home to Leeds. To add further spice to the day, City were now managed by Alan Ball who had left Southampton to link up with his old pal Francis Lee at Maine Road. It proved to be an agonising afternoon which started well enough as Cup finalists Liverpool raced into a 2-0 lead allowing Saints and Coventry fans to relax a little. However, City fought back to level and at this stage all three sides were drawing. Merrington's men did not know whether to "stick or twist". They could go forward and try to get the win which would make sure but that would risk leaving gaps knowing that if they conceded they would be down. Alternatively they could keep it tight at 0-0 at hope City did not get a late winner. The momentum was with City against a disinterested Liverpool side who were keen to avoid injuries ahead of the Cup Final. Remarkably, unlikely salvation came when Ball was wrongly told Saints were losing and that a draw was enough for his side. The order went out to play for a draw and Steve Lomas memorably took the ball to the corner flag to play out time when his side still needed another goal. City drew 2-2 while Saints and Coventry both finished 0-0 to survive ahead of them on goal difference. Merrington, the

Carling Manager of the Month, did not hang around to celebrate the triumph which was put into sharp perspective by news of his wife Pauline's serious illness. She had suffered a brain haemorrhage a few days before the game and her life was in the balance with the manager not knowing whether she would still be alive when he got back from the game. However, he left her bedside and went to The Dell, led his team to safety and then went straight back to the hospital. His reward – barely a month later – was the sack!

Premiership Table 1995-96

	P	W	D	L	F	A	Pts
Sheffield Wednesday	38	10	10	18	48	61	40
Coventry City	38	8	14	16	42	60	38
Southampton	38	9	11	18	34	52	38
Manchester City	38	9	11	18	33	58	38
Queens Park Rangers	38	8	6	23	38	57	33
Bolton Wanderers	38	5	5	25	39	71	29

FOSTER CARE

Lawrie McMenemy enlisted the help of fellow Geordie Brendan Foster in August 1974. The Olympic athlete took the Southampton squad running round the track at Gateshead before their match at Sunderland. It failed to pay off as Saints were beaten 3-1 despite taking the lead with a Mike Channon penalty.

RISING STAR

Theo Walcott became the youngest player ever to appear in a first-team game for Saints when he came off the bench against Wolves on August 6, 2005. He was aged 16 years and 143 days, beating the record held by Danny Wallace who was 16 and 313 days when he faced Manchester United on November 29, 1980. Walcott then became the youngest player ever to score for Saints when he netted in a 2-1 defeat at Leeds in October 2005. He is also the youngest player ever to appear for the reserves, aged 15 years and 175 days beating the previous record set by Andrew Surman who was 15 years and 196 days old when he came off the bench against Chelsea on March 4, 2002.

GREAT ESCAPES PART THREE: 1996-97

Under new boss Graeme Souness, Saints began the campaign brightly sweeping to a stunning 6-3 win over champions-elect Manchester United. Their inconsistency was highlighted just two games later when they crashed 7-1 at Everton. By the beginning of April, Saints were rooted to the foot of the Premiership with seven games left – starting with a do-or-die affair at relegation rivals Nottingham Forest. New signing from Plymouth Micky Evans repaid his £500,000 fee in one game scoring twice in a 3-1 win which proved a turning-point. Saints remained unbeaten until the final game of the campaign winning six-pointers against West Ham and Sunderland while drawing with fellow strugglers Coventry. Again their fate was in their own hands on the final day as they went to Villa needing a draw for survival against opposition who needed a point to get into Europe. It looked odds on to end all-square – but Saints lost 1-0 to a Richard Dryden own goal. However, scores elsewhere meant they were safe well before the end of the game.

Premiership Table 1996-97

	P	W	D	L	F	A	Pts
Blackburn Rovers	38	9	15	14	42	43	42
West Ham United	38	10	12	16	39	48	42
Everton	38	10	12	16	44	57	42
Southampton	38	10	11	17	50	56	41
Coventry City	38	9	14	15	38	54	41
Sunderland	38	10	10	18	35	53	40
Middlesbrough	38	10	12	16	51	60	39
Nottingham Forest	38	6	16	16	31	59	34

WORLD CUP STARS

Agustin Delgado became the first Saints player ever to score in the World Cup finals when he headed home for Ecuador after just five minutes of their group game against Mexico on June 9, 2002. Having waited 72 years for that moment, Saints had a second scorer just three days later when Sweden's Anders Svensson stunned Argentina with a magnificent free-kick for a 1-1 draw which put the South Americans out and ensured England went through.

GREAT ESCAPES PART FOUR: 1998-99

For many Saints fans this was the definitive Great Escape with Saints looking dead and buried for most of the season. They spent virtually the entire campaign in the bottom three, clambering out only in the last three games. Dave Jones' side lost seven of their first eight games of the campaign, drawing the other at home to Spurs. By the time they hosted Wimbledon on December 19 they had just 10 points from 17 games, with 11 defeats in that run. However, new Moroccan midfielder Hassan Kachloul inspired the side to a 3-1 win over the Dons to turn the season around. They lost their next game at home to Chelsea, but it was the last Dell defeat of the campaign. With five games to go they hosted relegation rivals Blackburn and trailed 3-1 after 61 minutes only to show huge character and earn a 3-3 draw which visibly knocked the stuffing out of Rovers, who would finish second from bottom. Even so, it still looked a tall order as Southampton went into the last three games in 19th place, and then fell behind at home to Leicester. They still trailed with 16 minutes remaining until Chris Marsden scored with a thumping header and James Beattie won it with a terrific cushioned volley from a tight angle. Blackburn's draw against Charlton, meant Saints pulled clear of the drop zone for the first time that season. A 2-0 win at Wimbledon followed, where they were roared on by an estimated 11,000 fans, to set up a tense final day at home to Everton. Saints were two points clear of Charlton who had a vastly superior goal difference. The Addicks needed to win and hope Saints could do no more than draw. However, Premiership status was confirmed with a 2-0 victory, thanks to a double from Marian Pahars. Charlton lost at home to Sheffield Wednesday leaving Saints some five points clear of danger.

Premiership Table 1998-99

	P	W	D	L	F	A	Pts
Everton	38	11	10	17	42	47	43
Coventry City	38	11	9	18	39	51	42
Wimbledon	38	10	12	16	40	63	42
Southampton	38	11	8	19	37	64	41
Charlton Athletic	38	8	12	18	41	56	36
Blackburn Rovers	38	7	14	17	38	52	35
Nottingham Forest	38	7	9	22	35	69	30

TRANMERE TROUBLE

The last ever cup-tie at The Dell was a dismal goalless draw against Tranmere who were then fighting relegation from the second tier of English football. It was 102 years to the week since the old ground staged its first cup-tie and it was an unremarkable affair apart from an injury-time "winner" from Wayne Bridge being disallowed for a foul on the keeper. The replay at Prenton Park could hardly have been more different: packed with drama and still etched painfully into the memories of most Saints fans even now. Unusually, the 10-day replay rule was waived by the police to avoid clashing with the following week's international break and the second game was staged just three days after the first. That meant Jason Dodd and Matthew Oakley did not have time to recover from injuries received on the Saturday – but it seemed not to matter as a rampant Saints side raced into a 3-0 interval lead with goals by Hassan Kachloul, Jo Tessem and Dean Richards. Tranmere were renowned as cup upset specialists, particularly in home midweek games. But they barely mounted an attack in a one-sided first half before staging one of the biggest fight-backs in the competition's history. Glenn Hoddle felt confident enough at 3-0 to withdraw Latvian duo Marian Pahars and Imants Bleidelis and for the first 13 minutes of the second half the game meandered towards a seemingly inevitable conclusion. Even when former Saints striker Paul Rideout forced home from close range following a corner, there should not have been any major problem. But the travelling fans could sense an unease in their side who suddenly looked shaky and the home crowd felt it too. They pumped up the volume and urged on their team, who found new momentum. Rideout was given a free header for his side's second on 70 minutes and suddenly it was backs-to-the-wall for an increasingly fragile Saints side whose fans were already hoping they could just hang on for penalties even with a one-goal advantage. That was wiped out nine minutes later when Rideout rocked his old club by completing a quickfire hat-trick. And with just five minutes remaining Stuart Barlow nicked a dramatic winner to complete Southampton's humiliation live on TV with Hoddle describing it as his worst moment in football.

GREAT ESCAPE: THE RE-MAKE

After four final-day escapes, Saints' luck finally ran out in 2005 when they lost 2-1 at home to Manchester United and finished bottom of the table for the first time in their history. It ended a proud 27-year stay in the top-flight – but surely it would also spell an end to survival struggles? Not so, three years after dropping into the Coca-Cola Championship Saints found themselves battling to stay in a division they had spent years trying to avoid! The risk of relegation crept up by stealth. For the first half of the campaign Saints harboured hopes of making the play-offs but even when they lost manager George Burley to Scotland, there did not seem any major cause for panic. Then suddenly, with five games left to play, they dropped into the bottom three. By now Nigel Pearson was in charge and he inspired a strong response. His side comprehensively beat promotion-chasing Bristol City and then drew at Charlton. It looked as though the scare had been averted but a shock 1-0 home defeat by Burnley meant a grim finale. Saints were in the drop zone as they went to West Brom who needed a point for promotion – and they almost snatched an unlikely victory when Adam Lallana scored his first league goal for the club 12 minutes from time. But, with six minutes remaining, Chris Brunt equalised to leave Southampton's fate out of their own hands on the last day. To make matters even harder, opponents Sheffield United were the form team of the division after a run which had given them an unlikely chance of making the play-offs. With a vastly inferior goal difference, Pearson's men had to do better than Leicester or win and hope that Coventry or Blackpool lost. They fell behind to a Stephen Quinn goal but levelled just before the break with Marek Saganowski's first goal since September. Stern John fired them in front but the home crowd were stunned into silence when Jon Stead levelled. Almost immediately the lead was restored by John who was sent off 10 minutes from time for a second yellow card – the first for taking his shirt off in celebration. Saints hung on grimly and Leicester went down to the third tier for the first time in their history despite an impressive 0-0 draw at Stoke who clinched promotion as a result. Coventry collapsed 4-1 at Charlton but just stayed up.

Championship Table 2007-08

	P	W	D	L	F	A	Pts
19 Blackpool	46	12	18	16	59	64	54
20 Southampton	46	13	15	18	56	72	54
21 Coventry	46	14	11	21	52	64	53
22 Leicester	46	12	16	18	42	45	52
23 Scunthorpe	46	11	13	22	46	69	46
24 Colchester	46	7	17	22	62	86	38

TOP GUN

Alan Shearer became the youngest player ever to score a top-flight hat-trick when he netted three times in Saints' 4-2 win over Arsenal in April 1988. He was only told he was playing a couple of hours before kick-off to ensure he did not have time to get nervous – and it took him just five minutes to mark his first senior start with a goal, heading in from five yards. An own goal by Kevin Bond brought the visitors level six minutes later only for Shearer to stoop and nod his second on 33 minutes. Mark Blake made it 3-1 at the break and Shearer completed his treble four minutes into the second half. His initial shot came back off the underside of the bar but the youngster reacted quickest to force home the rebound, showing the first signs of what was to come in a glorious career. Paul Davis got a late consolation for the Gunners but the headlines belonged to Shearer who, at 17 years and 240 days, became the youngest player to net a hat-trick in the top division, breaking a 30-year record held by the great Jimmy Greaves.

VAN THE MAN

Saints signed man-mountain Uli Van Gobbel for £1.5m in October 1996. The Dutch defender followed Graeme Souness from Galatasaray and became something of a cult hero among the fans for his power and build. However, he struggled to adapt to the Premiership and returned to his former club Feyenoord in August 1997. He retired in 2002 but fled Holland after receiving a four-month jail sentence for buying cars on credit and selling them on without paying the car company. He is believed to have settled in his native Surinam.

TWO ON TRIAL

In September 1996, Saints gave a closed doors trial to two Norwegian unknowns – Egil Ostenstad and Tore Andre Flo. Both looked sensational and wheels were set in motion to secure the pair. Ostenstad duly signed from Viking Stavanger for £900,000 but Saints failed to agree terms for Flo because of a complicated deal which would involve his old club getting a cut of the fee. He went on to carve out a hugely successful career with Chelsea while Ostenstad netted 33 goals in 92 appearances before moving to Blackburn in an exchange deal which saw Kevin Davies return to The Dell.

THREE FOR JOY

Saints finished tenth in 1994-95, but owed much to a home game against Newcastle which proved a significant turning point in the campaign. After a promising start to the season Alan Ball's side had dropped into the relegation zone after a run of 12 games without a win. Paul Kitson gave the Magpies a 12th-minute advantage and the visitors were still leading 1-0 with four minutes remaining. The midweek match looked to be petering to a sad conclusion, which would have left Saints in real trouble, until a sensational fight-back saw them score three times, including two in injury-time. First Neil Heaney prodded home from close range and as the home crowd pumped up the volume, Gordon Watson capitalised on a spill by Pavel Srnicek and then Neil Shipperley flicked in the third following another fumble by the keeper. Saints went on to win five and draw three of their next 10, the only defeats coming at Liverpool and Manchester United as they secured their first top-half finish since 1990.

SILLETT BANG!

Former skipper Charlie Sillett was middleweight boxing champion of the Kings Royal Rifle Corps for three years before he signed from Tidworth where he had been stationed as an Army PT instructor. He was most effective at full-back but also played up front and in midfield. He left the club for non-league Guildford City in 1938.

EVERTON EXITS

Dave Jones' last match in charge of Saints was a 2-0 win at home to Everton before he was replaced by Glenn Hoddle – whose final game was also at home to the Goodison Park outfit some 14 months later. He signed off with a 1-0 victory.

JAW-DROPPING MOMENT

In August 1988 Saints won their first three games of the season for the first time since 1957 as they beat West Ham 4-0 at The Dell then secured a 1-0 victory at QPR before polishing off visitors Luton 2-1. They then went to Arsenal looking to set a new club record by winning four in a row at the start of the season for the first time since they joined the Football League in 1920. And to this day, many fans feels they were cheated out of it. Chris Nicholl's flamboyant young side, playing an adventurous 4-2-4 system, raced into a 2-0 lead in just 24 minutes with goals from Matthew Le Tissier and Rod Wallace. The Gunners never looked a threat until they were literally handed a penalty eight minutes from time when Kevin Moore was penalised for handball. Brian Marwood tucked it away to set up a tense finale but Saints were still in front at 90 minutes. However, Southend referee David Axcell added on an astonishing nine minutes of injury-time, presumably to penalise Saints for time-wasting. He believed Glenn Cockerill was trying to run down the clock as he went down clutching his face. Television replays showed a sly punch by Arsenal midfielder Paul Davis that broke Cockerill's jaw in two places. He received a record nine-match ban and a £3,000 fine. However, it proved that crime does pay as seven minutes into the added time Alan Smith scored an equaliser which was to prove crucial at the end of the season when Arsenal memorably won the title at Anfield on goal difference!

PENALTY KINGS.

Saints' first experience of settling a cup-tie from the spot came in 1985 when they beat Millwall 5-4 in the second round of the Milk Cup (League Cup) after both legs had finished 0-0.

THREE'S A CROWD

Saints were the first victims of the new "three up, three down" system in 1974. Previously only two teams had ever been relegated each season in the top-flight but in a move designed to add excitement to Divisions 1 and 2, that changed – and Saints suffered. They were fifth in mid-December but won only two of their next 21 games, sliding into the bottom three for the first time in the final week of the campaign. They lost 3-0 at Burnley and rivals Birmingham beat QPR 4-0 the following night to leave Lawrie McMenemy's men needing to win their final game at Everton, and then hope that the Midlands side would fail to beat already-relegated Norwich. Saints did their bit, winning 3-0 at Goodison Park where they had previously only ever won once. But Birmingham beat the Canaries 2-1 to stay up by a point.

READY RESPONSE

After FA Cup hero Bobby Stokes hung up his boots, he fell on hard times. His friends rallied round for a fund-raising effort which included sending a standard letter to major sportswear firms asking for help. It began: "At **4.37pm** on May 1, 1976 Bobby Stokes ran through a static Manchester United defence to score the most important goal in Southampton's history…" He duly received a reply which read: "At **4.37pm** on May 1, 1976 I was part of a Manchester United defence which waited in vain for an offside flag which never came… Yours sincerely, Martin Buchan."

PARK KEEPER

Goalkeeper Len Stansbridge made the pitch his own, first as a player and then as head groundsman. He came through the youth ranks to make his senior debut in a 2-0 defeat at Plymouth in the final game of 1938-39 season but his career was interrupted by the Second World War. He spent much of it as a prisoner of war in Germany but returned to The Dell in 1946 to understudy George Ephgrave. He made a total of 48 appearances before moving to Basingstoke. He returned to The Dell in 1962 as groundsman and tended the pitch until his retirement in May 1984. He died two years later.

A DOUBLE TO START AND A DOUBLE TO FINISH

Hassan Kachloul scored twice in a 2-2 draw at Derby on the opening day of the 2000-01 season – and he netted another double in the final game of the season, a 3-2 win over Arsenal in the last league game at The Dell. But, he did not find the net at all in his 24 other league appearances of the campaign.

NOT MUCH CHARITY

Saints' solitary appearance in the FA Charity Shield came in August 1976 as a result of their FA Cup win over Manchester United. This time there was no upset as Lawrie McMenemy's men went down 1-0 to Champions Liverpool thanks to a John Toshack goal on 50 minutes.

NOT SO SUPER CUP

Saints qualified for the UEFA Cup in 1985 but found themselves banned through no fault of their own. The tragic events at the Liverpool v Juventus European Cup Final at Heysel Stadium in Brussels that May, meant that all English clubs were kicked out of Europe in a blanket punishment. As a poor consolation, and to help compensate for the loss of revenue, the Screen Sport Super Cup was introduced with two groups of three. Southampton found themselves in with Tottenham and Liverpool losing both away legs 2-1 then drawing 1-1 at home to the Anfield aces before losing 3-1 to Spurs at The Dell in front of just 4,680 fans.

TRIBUNAL TRIBULATIONS

Saints' first experience of the new tribunal system to set fees for free agents came in 1987 when centre-back Jon Gittens exercised his freedom of contract. He had signed from non-league Paget Rangers and showed plenty of raw potential but opted to move to Swindon. The fee was set at a paltry £40,000. Four years later, manager Chris Nicholl paid 10 times that amount to bring him back but it was not a success and 15 months later he moved to Middlesbrough with Saints taking a £50,000 loss.

BLACKBURN BASH-ED

Steve Basham scored his only goal for Saints in the 2-0 win at Blackburn in November 1998. Matthew Oakley opened the scoring and Basham came off the bench to seal a vital victory in injury-time, bundling his way past two defenders before curling the ball home. It proved crucial come the end of the season with Saints completing another Great Escape at the expense of Blackburn, who were relegated.

DON AND DUSTED

Saints' 2-0 win at home to Wimbledon on the final day of the 1999-2000 season relegated the Dons. Wayne Bridge scored his first senior goal with a powerful free-kick and Marian Pahars added a second following a 60-yard solo run. Bradford's victory over Liverpool ensured the south London side went down.

GOAL OF THE SEASON

Matthew Le Tissier won the BBC Goal of the Season competition in 1994-95 for his sensational strike in a 3-2 defeat at Blackburn. He picked up Tommy Widdrington's pass just outside the centre circle and weaved left then right before unleashing a stunning 35-yard shot into the top left corner past his old pal Tim Flowers who knew it was coming but was totally unable to get near it such was the power and precision. Even the home fans applauded!

HITTING THE ROOF

Saints were involved in the first ever 'indoor' FA Cup Final in 2003. Heavy pre-match rain meant the roof at the Millennium Stadium was closed for the first time at an FA Cup final. It added to a crackling atmosphere, trapping the noise from the hordes of Saints fans who formed a huge wall of yellow at one end of the stadium. Although Southampton lost 1-0 to a Robert Pires goal, they emerged with huge credit for the sportsmanship of the supporters who stayed to applaud the Gunners and to cheer their own side off despite the bitter disappointment.

WATER IN THE RADIO?

In one of the early live Sky games, Saints went to Tottenham in February 1993 and looked to be cruising at 1-0 thanks to an Iain Dowie goal. They were comfortably in control and one Saints fan, out for a Sunday drive, memorably decided to put his car through a car wash. He lowered the aerial with his side still leading – and came out the other end to find they were 4-1 down! In the space of five minutes Ian Branfoot's men had conceded four goals to Teddy Sheringham (54), Nicky Barmby (56), Darren Anderton (57) and Sheringham again (58). Francis Benali was sent off on the hour for a horrendous tackle before Richard Hall headed in a Matthew Le Tissier corner six minutes later.

UNABLE TO 'OLD 'EM

Saints were safe from the threat of relegation when they went to Oldham for the final game of the 1992-93 season – but the Latics were still in desperate danger. They had to beat Southampton and hope that rivals Crystal Palace lost at Arsenal. The Gunners duly obliged with a 3-0 win but Ian Branfoot's men put the Boundary Park crowd through hell by making a real fight of it. Matthew Le Tissier quickly cancelled out Neil Pointon's early opener before the Lancashire side raced into a seemingly unassailable 4-1 lead with goals by Andy Ritchie, Ian Olney and Gunnar Halle. But Le Tissier pulled one back on 67 minutes and completed his second hat-trick for the club with six minutes remaining. Saints went for it through seemingly interminable stoppage time but Joe Royle's battlers held on to send Palace down on goal difference.

SHILTON SCORES

Saints goalkeeper Campbell Forsyth was left red-faced as his opposite number scored a fluke goal with an extraordinary drop-kick at The Dell in October 1967. Saints were already 4-1 down to Leicester City when Peter Shilton launched a clearance which bounced in front of Forsyth who could only watch in horror as the ball bounced over him and into the net to complete a 5-1 win for the visitors.

THE JOY OF SIX – SIX HITTERS

1. In his debut season in Division One, Ron Davies was neck and neck at the top of the goalscoring charts with World Cup winner Geoff Hurst until the final game of the campaign. Saints thumped already relegated Aston Villa 6-2 at The Dell with Martin Chivers scoring two and Davies grabbing four. Already way out in front as the division's top scorer with a remarkable 37 goals, Davies was now two goals clear of Hurst in all competitions.

Player	Club	Lge	FA	LC	Total
Davies	Saints	37	3	3	43
Hurst	W Ham	29	3	9	41
Greaves	Spurs	25	6	0	31

2. Chelsea had never previously conceded six at home until Saints went to Stamford Bridge in September 1967 and won 6-2 with four goals by Ron Davies and two from Martin Chivers.

3. The stay-away fans missed a treat as Saints thrashed Crystal Palace 6-0 at The Dell in the final game of the 1970-71 season. The crowd of 15,980 was the club's smallest top-flight attendance to date but they were rewarded with two strikes by Mike Channon and one each from Jimmy Gabriel, Brian O'Neil, Ron Davies and home debutant Les Harfield – his only goal for the club. Saints finished seventh and with the "one club, one city" rule being retained once more, Ted Bates' side qualified for the Fairs Cup for the second time in three seasons.

4. When Manchester United lost 5-1 at Newcastle in October 1996, many an 'expert' predicted it would be a long time before they conceded that many again. It took six days to be precise as Saints thumped them 6-3 at The Dell. Egil Ostenstad scored what most Southampton fans still regard as a hat-trick even though he had his final goal chalked off as an own goal by the Premier League dubious goals panel. Eyal Berkovic rammed in a double and Matthew Le Tissier lobbed Peter Schmeichel with a carbon copy of the goal Phillipe Albert had scored for Newcastle the previous week.

5. Southampton's biggest win at St Mary's is a Worthington League Cup tie against Tranmere Rovers, which brought a 6-1 victory in October 2002. Striker Brett Ormerod bagged a hat-trick with the other goals coming from Chris Marsden, Fabrice Fernandes and Michael Svensson.

6. Even the most ardent Saints fan could not have envisaged the outcome as their side travelled to Wolves in March 2007. Ravaged by injury and suspension, they were missing their entire regular back four and keeper Kelvin Davis. But somehow they pulled off a sensational 6-0 win. Wolves probably had more of the play and looked the better team but every Southampton shot (apart from one) went in. Marek Saganowski helped himself to a hat-trick with the others coming from Leon Best, Andrew Surman and a Gary Breen own goal. It was the first time they had hit six on the road since winning by the same score at Carlisle in January 1977 with two goals by Nick Holmes and one each from David Peach, Ted MacDougall, Mike Channon and Peter Osgood.

GERMAN MARK

Uwe Rosler holds the distinction of scoring the last ever goal at The Dell. Although Matthew Le Tissier memorably netted the last league goal, the East German international got the only strike of the game in the farewell friendly against Brighton who had also been the first ever opponents at The Dell. Rosler had been snapped up on a free transfer when his club Tennis Borussia Berlin went bankrupt in July 2000. But, hampered by a persistent groin problem, he struggled to hold down a regular place and moved to German Second Division side Unterhaching in January 2002. He moved into Norwegian football and successfully won his hardest battle, beating lung cancer – despite initial internet reports which claimed he had died.

RECORD FEE

Saints' record transfer fee paid remains the £4m shelled out to Derby for versatile midfielder Rory Delap in July 2001.

HIT FOR SIX – SIX SPANKINGS

1. When Saints lost 6-0 at home to Brentford in March 1959 it set a new post-war record for the club. It was their heaviest home defeat since Plymouth won by the same score in December 1931.

2. Saints last scored 100 league goals in 1963-64, a campaign which saw them hit six against Charlton, Grimsby, Derby and Rotherham and seven against Scunthorpe. It was 10 goals more than any other club in the division. However, they finished only fifth because only six clubs conceded more. One of those was Swansea who just avoided the drop thanks to a thumping 6-0 win over Saints.

3. Having topped the table in early 1982, Saints were rocked by the summer departure of Kevin Keegan – but signed England keeper Peter Shilton from Nottingham Forest. However, they made a wretched start to the 1982-83 campaign losing five and drawing one of their first seven league games. That run included a 5-0 hammering at Anfield, a 4-1 defeat at Watford and a 6-0 thrashing at Spurs who also missed a penalty. It was Southampton's heaviest league defeat for eight years and a torrid baptism of fire for the new keeper.

4. Saints hated playing on plastic pitches and crashed 6-1 on Luton's horrible artificial surface on January 2, 1989, a terrible start to the New Year. Rod Wallace got the consolation with a fine solo effort.

5. Chris Nicholl's fate as manager was sealed by a woeful display in their penultimate game of the 1990-91 season at bottom club Derby who had long since been relegated with close to a record low number of points. Southampton put up barely any resistance as they were swamped 6-2 with future Saints defender Paul Williams bagging an unlikely hat-trick. Nicholl was sacked not long after the final game of the season, a 1-1 draw at home to Wimbledon which saw Jimmy Case score his final goal for the club.

6. Ten days before meeting Arsenal in the 2003 FA Cup Final, Saints visited Highbury for a "dress rehearsal" which could scarcely

have gone any worse. They were hit by five goals in the space of 17 minutes and although Jo Tessem pulled one back just before the break, Robert Pires netted again two minutes into the second half to complete his treble – although he had already been beaten to a hat-trick by Jermaine Pennant.

ANTTI POST

Saints were trailing 2-1 in a Barclays Premier League game at Fulham in March 2003 when they won a corner three minutes into stoppage time. Goalkeeper Antti Niemi sprinted up field and was not spotted by the defence, despite his bright orange jersey. The Finnish international showed terrific technique as the ball came to him, chesting and then volleying against a post. Michael Svensson stooped to head the rebound into the empty net to salvage a point.

STRETCHERED – OFF!

Jimmy Gabriel was sent off while on a stretcher towards the end of the 1-0 defeat at Leeds in 1970. The hard-man defender "clashed heads" with striker Allan Clarke who fell to the ground. Gabriel went down too in the hope of avoiding punishment but the referee saw it as a head-butt and dismissed him as he was being carried off. He looked set for a lengthy ban but the referee's report was vague and contradictory and the FA disciplinary committee seemed more interested in breaking for lunch than holding a potentially-lengthy hearing. They agreed to a plea bargain where Gabriel admitted guilt but they decided the sending-off was sufficient punishment!

TRAGIC LOSS

Darting forward Austin Hayes showed plenty of early promise scoring twice on his debut, a 4-1 win at home to Carrick Rangers in the Cup Winners Cup in November 1976. He went on to play for Ireland and appeared for Saints in the 1979 League Cup Final but he could not command a regular place and moved to Millwall for £50,000 in February 1981. His life was tragically cut short by cancer and he died in December 1986 aged just 38.

NOT MUCH BETWEEN THE SIDES

In March 1992, Saints embarked on a run of six successive wins – all by a single goal margin. They won 1-0 at home to both West Ham and Crystal Palace with goals by Iain Dowie and Matthew Le Tissier, respectively. They then won by the same score at Man City with Dowie again on target. Goals by Dowie and Alan Shearer brought a 2-1 victory at home to Luton and then Glenn Cockerill netted the only goal of the game at Everton before QPR were dispatched 2-1 at The Dell by another Shearer/Dowie combo. The sequence was ended by Forest who won at The Dell – almost inevitably the score was 1-0. Normal service was resumed with a 1-0 win at West Ham thanks to Micky Adams. And so it continued… Saints lost 1-0 at Manchester United and then at home to Sheffield Wednesday, but then won 1-0 at Wimbledon and at home to Oldham. That made it a run of 12 successive games decided by just one goal – or 13 if you count the 3-2 defeat in extra-time in the Zenith Data Systems Cup Final at Wembley. The sequence was smashed in the final game of the season as they crashed 5-1 at Arsenal where victory would have seen them climb to 11th instead of finishing life in the old First Division in 16th place.

BEGIN WITH A BANG

Southampton-born striker Nicky Banger celebrated his first-team debut with a hat-trick in a Rumbelows League Cup tie against Rochdale in October 1990. Saints already had the tie won thanks to a 5-0 away-leg win with two goals by Alan Shearer and one apiece from Barry Horne, Rod Wallace and Neil Ruddock. That gave Chris Nicholl the freedom to blood the young prospect who had been banging in the goals for the youth and Reserve teams. He lived up to his name with all three in a 3-0 win. He then dropped back to the Reserves and when he did get a chance, it was normally as a substitute. He made just 21 starts and 41 appearances from the bench netting eight league goals before moving to Oldham where injury hampered his career. He had spells at clubs as far apart as Hearts, Bournemouth, Dundee and Plymouth before returning to join ambitious Eastleigh where he played and worked on the commercial side. He also presented a show on The Saint, the radio station owned by Southampton FC and based at St Mary's.

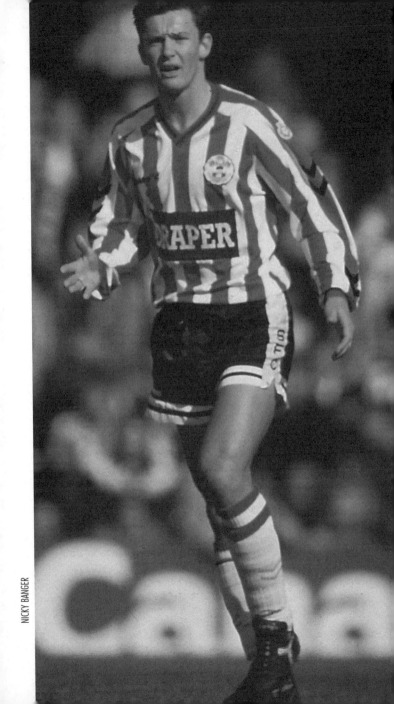

NICKY BANGER

DIVISION ONE AT LAST

After 45 years in the Football League and 81 in existence, Southampton Football Club finally made it to the top tier of English Football in 1966. It was a complete contrast to 1948-49 when they led the Second Division for most of the season only to miss out at the death. This time Saints crept up on the rails. When they lost 1-0 at home to Birmingham on March 5 they were down in fifth place and with no real expectation among the fans that this would prove to be the most magical year of their lives, especially as a World Cup win soon followed! In the wake of that defeat, Ted Bates strengthened the defence by signing David Webb from Orient with George O'Brien going the other way. It proved an inspired switch. Webb scored on his debut, a 1-1 draw at Wolves, and played in every remaining fixture as Saints strung together a 12-match unbeaten run. With five matches remaining Saints were still fifth but with two games in hand following two postponements, and four of the five were away from home. They drew 1-1 at Preston then beat Charlton 1-0 at The Dell before going to Plymouth where they trailed 2-1. Denis Hollywood scored his first ever goal for the club and Jimmy Melia netted a winner while recent leaders Huddersfield lost at home to Coventry who were playing their last fixture of the campaign. In those days there was no requirement for all clubs to play their final game at the same time so Saints had the advantage of knowing exactly what was needed – one point from two games, provided they did not concede a lot of goals. They were further helped when Leyton Orient agreed to put the match back by a week because Alf Ramsey had refused to release Terry Paine from the England squad for a friendly against Yugoslavia in preparation for the World Cup. Paine's presence was to prove vital as – fittingly – he headed the equaliser in a 1-1 draw at Brisbane Road watched by 12,000 travelling fans who invaded the pitch in joy. Bates was cautious of celebrating too soon, knowing that a six-goal defeat at champions Manchester City would see the long-awaited promotion place slip from the grasp. City were in party mood after picking up the trophy before kick-off and Saints were never in danger of losing as they closed out a 0-0 draw. First Division football was about to become a reality!

Second Division Table 1965-66

	P	W	D	L	F	A	P
Manchester City	42	22	15	5	76	44	59
Southampton	42	22	10	10	85	56	54
Coventry City	42	20	13	9	73	53	53
Huddersfield Town	42	19	13	10	62	36	51
Bristol City	42	17	17	8	63	48	51

DIA DECISION

Graeme Souness will never live down the embarrassing episode in November 1996 when he took a phone call offering him a "talented" youngster by the name of Ali Dia. The striker was supposedly highly recommended by World Footballer of the Year George Weah; there was even a suggestion that Dia was a cousin of the player. He did not look anything special in training but an injury crisis meant a short-term contract was hastily drawn up and the unknown found himself on the bench for a home game against Leeds. After 32 minutes, Matthew Le Tissier limped off and Souness sent on the Senegalese striker who, it later emerged, had been rejected at both Bournemouth and Gillingham. Almost immediately he raced clean through one-on-one and might have made himself a hero but he was denied by a smart save from Nigel Martyn. After that it quickly became obvious he was out of his depth as he chased around like a headless chicken before being substituted himself five minutes from time after his 53 minutes of fame. Not surprisingly, he was released the following week and later played for Gateshead and Spennymoor.

RECORD CROWD

Saints' highest ever attendance at St Mary's is 32,151 for the 1-0 home defeat by Arsenal in December 2003. Their biggest attendance at The Dell was 31,044 who packed in to see the 3-0 defeat by Manchester United in October 1969. That remained a club record until the move to St Mary's when the opening league game at the new stadium drew a crowd of 31,107. Big crowds do not seem to suit Saints as once again they lost, this time 2-0 to Chelsea.

BOXING DAY DISAPPOINTMENTS

There has not been much Christmas cheer for Saints who have won only one Boxing Day fixture since beating Wimbledon at The Dell in 1993. Their sole December 26 success in that spell was a 1-0 victory at home to Spurs in 2001 with a goal by James Beattie in a game which saw returning duo Glenn Hoddle and Dean Richards booed throughout. Saints had also beaten Tottenham in a festive fixture the previous year, but that 2-0 win was on December 27 with Beattie and Kevin Davies netting.

Year	Opponent	Score
2007	Colchester United (a)	1-1
2006	Crystal Palace (h)	1-1
2005	Watford (a)	0-3
2004	Charlton Athletic (h)	0-0
2003	Fulham (a)	0-2
2002	Chelsea (a)	0-0
2001	Tottenham Hotspur (h)	1-0
2000	No fixture: played December 27	
1999	Chelsea (h)	1-2
1998	Chelsea (h)	0-2
1997	Crystal Palace (a)	1-1
1996	Tottenham Hotspur (a)	1-3
1995	Tottenham Hotspur (h)	0-0
1994	Wimbledon (h)	2-3

TURF AT THE TOP

Saints had grounds for celebration in 2004, and again in 2008, when they won a pitch battle for the title of Groundsman of the Year. In 2004, Dave Roberts won the Barclays Premier League trophy for the best-kept pitch and his successor Andy Gray and Graeme Mills won the Coca-Cola Championship award four years later with their team of Ricky Rawlins, Danny Silvestri and Dan Osborne. Saints have been nominated in the top three for whichever division they have been ever since the move to St Mary's – apart from the first season, 2001-02, when it was still bedding down.

OH BOYER!

Phil Boyer scored in 10 consecutive home league games between the 3-2 win over Liverpool on September 1, 1979 and the 2-0 victory against Bolton on December 29 of the same year.

DOUBLE DUTCH

Saints appointed their first foreign boss on May 30, 2008 when Jan Poortvliet was unveiled as the new head coach in tandem with fellow Dutchman Mark Wotte. Poortvliet played right-back for the Netherlands in the 1978 World Cup Final defeat by hosts Argentina while Wotte is a former technical director at Feyenoord. The pair succeeded Nigel Pearson whose contract was not renewed despite leading the side to Coca-Cola Championship safety on the final day of the season. The Dutch duo would be working closely with reserve boss Stewart Henderson and Under 18s coach Dave Hockaday in a new-look continental-style set-up designed to ensure a seamless transition from the youth team to the senior side.

RAPID PROGRESS

It took just five days for Saints to progress from the last 16 of the FA Cup to a semi-final in 1986. After drawing 0-0 at home to Millwall on February 15, Chris Nicholl's men had to wait until March 3 for the replay at The Den where Danny Wallace scored the only goal. On March 8, Saints won 2-0 in the quarter-final at Brighton with goals by Steve Moran and Glenn Cockerill. Suddenly they were looking forward to a semi-final against mighty Liverpool at White Hart Lane. Nicholl's men battled bravely against the champions-elect – despite the bitter blow of losing Mark Wright with a broken leg after 39 minutes. The England centre-back collided with his own goalkeeper Peter Shilton as they chased a through-ball and there was a horrible crunch. Player reactions immediately signified he was badly hurt. It proved to be a broken fibula which ended his hopes of playing for England in the World Cup finals. Somehow Saints held the mighty Merseysiders to 0-0 after 90 minutes but the loss of Wright proved decisive in extra-time with Liverpool winning 2-0 with an Ian Rush double.

SLOW STARTERS

Saints have been slow starters over the past two decades, winning their opening game only once in 20 years. On August 27 1988 they thumped West Ham 4-0 but their only other win was a 1-0 success at Coventry on August 7 1999 when Egil Ostenstad netted the only goal.

1988	West Ham (h)	4-0
1989	Millwall (h)	1-2
1990	Aston Villa (a)	1-1
1991	Tottenham Hotspur (h)	2-3
1992	Tottenham Hotspur (h)	0-0
1993	Everton (a)	0-2
1994	Blackburn Rovers (h)	1-1
1995	Nottingham Forest (h)	3-4
1996	Chelsea (h)	0-0
1997	Bolton Wanderers (h)	0-1
1998	Liverpool (h)	1-2
1999	Coventry City (a)	1-0
2000	Derby County (a)	2-2
2001	Leeds United (a)	0-2
2002	Middlesbrough (h)	0-0
2003	Leicester City (a)	2-2
2004	Aston Villa (a)	0-2
2005	Wolves (h)	0-0
2006	Derby (a)	2-2
2007	Crystal Palace (h)	1-4
2008	Cardiff City (a)	1-2

SCORING GOALS ISN'T ROCKET SCIENCE

Or rather it is… for Iain Dowie at least. The former Saints striker used to be a rocket scientist. After being rejected by Southampton as a schoolboy, he gained a degree in Engineering at the University of Hertfordshire and worked with British Aerospace, playing for St Albans and Hendon before joining Luton. From there he moved to West Ham. In September 1991, they sold him to Southampton who paid £500,000 for a player they had once released.

IAN DOWIE

POOLS COUPON KINGS

Saints became bankers for the Pools coupon in 2005 as they chalked up a club record run of eight successive league draws before losing 2-1 at Leeds. One more would have set an outright league record but – perhaps fittingly – they only equalled it. The defeat at Leeds left Saints level with Birmingham, Peterborough, Middlesbrough and Torquay.

Date	Opponent	Score
Aug 29	Coventry City (a)	1-1
Sept 10	QPR (h)	1-1
Sept 13	Ipswich Town (a)	2-2
Sept 18	Derby County (a)	2-2
Sept 24	Plymouth Argyle (h)	0-0
Sept 28	Reading (h)	0-0
Oct 1	Preston North End (a)	1-1
Oct 15	Hull City (h)	1-1

TREBLE TOP

The first hat-trick at St Mary's was scored by Craig Richards for Southampton Schools in a George Reader Trophy game in October 2001. The defender, from Bitterne Park School, went on to sign professional forms but suffered a badly broken leg which hampered his career.

PLAYER OF THE YEAR

In recent years, sponsors and supporters groups have added their own Player of the Year awards – but the traditional trophy is the one presented by the *Southern Daily Echo* and voted for by the fans. It dates back to Mike Channon as the inaugural winner in 1974 and, curiously, the first 11 winners were outfield players who slotted neatly into a team, plus a substitute. It just needed a goalkeeper to complete an outstanding line-up – Peter Shilton duly obliging in 1985 – and again the following year. He became the first of five keepers to win the award. Traditionally, Saints fans have liked to share the honour around with only Shilton, Tim Flowers, Matthew Le Tissier and James Beattie winning it more than once. The award somehow eluded such popular figures as Francis Benali, Jason Dodd, Ken Monkou, Danny Wallace and – perhaps most surprisingly – Nick Holmes.

1974	Mike Channon
1975	Mel Blyth
1976	David Peach
1977	Steve Williams
1978	Alan Ball
1979	Malcolm Waldron
1980	Phil Boyer
1981	Ivan Golac
1982	Kevin Keegan
1983	Mark Wright
1984	David Armstrong
1985	Peter Shilton
1986	Peter Shilton
1987	Glenn Cockerill
1988	Derek Statham
1989	Jimmy Case
1990	Matt Le Tissier
1991	Alan Shearer
1992	Tim Flowers
1993	Tim Flowers
1994	Matt Le Tissier
1995	Matt Le Tissier
1996	Dave Beasant
1997	Egil Ostenstad
1998	Paul Jones
1999	James Beattie
2000	Dean Richards
2001	Wayne Bridge
2002	Chris Marsden
2003	James Beattie
2004	Antti Niemi
2005	Peter Crouch
2006	Claus Lundekvam
2007	Chris Baird
2008	Andrew Davies

BEST CUP TEAM IN HAMPSHIRE

Saints have a 100 per cent success record against local rivals Pompey in the FA Cup. The teams first met in the competition in January 1906 when Southern League Saints romped to a 5-1 win despite fielding their third-choice keeper. Two goals by Harry Brown and one each from Fred Harrison, George Hedley and J Tomlinson set Saints en route to the quarter-finals. It was to be another 78 years before the Hampshire rivals were paired together in the competition again so there was a huge air of anticipation as they lined up at Fratton Park in January 1984. It is a day which will live long in the memories of all Saints fans lucky enough to be there – or those who have had the story told to them on countless occasions. There was a horribly hostile atmosphere which saw black striker Danny Wallace racially abused and pelted with bananas, while the rest of the team had coins thrown at them. Early in the second half, Mark Dennis was felled by an object thrown from the crowd as he prepared to take a throw-in. He recovered to play on and, fittingly, justice was done as Saints grabbed the only goal of the game in the time added on for the stoppage. David Armstrong crossed from the right and Steve Moran stole in at the far post to steer in a half-volley – both players hitting the ball with their weaker foot. Three sides of the ground were stunned into silence, Saints fans celebrated wildly and manager Lawrie McMenemy came up with the immortal quote: "We've had a great day. We have come away with two pounds of fruit, five pounds in loose change and a place in the last 16 of the Cup." Twelve years later the sides were paired together in the third round with Pompey making their first FA Cup visit to The Dell for 90 years. There was none of the drama of the Fratton Park encounter as Dave Merrington's men ran out comfortable 3-0 winners with Jim Magilton forcing home on 12 minutes and then again straight after half-time. Neil Shipperley rounded off a tame high noon shoot-out 10 minutes from time. By the time Portsmouth were next drawn against their local rivals in January 2005, Saints had moved to a new home – but the outcome remained the same. Matthew Oakley put Southampton in front on 54 minutes only for Yakubu to level with a controversial penalty three minutes later. The fourth round tie looked to be heading for a replay at Fratton Park until stoppage-time when the home side were awarded a spot-kick of their own. Showing enormous bottle, Peter Crouch stepped up against his former club and calmly slotted the winner – revealing afterwards he had had taken tips from penalty king Matt Le Tissier, beating him in a shoot-out for a television feature. Pompey have fared no better in the League Cup. The south coast sides have met in the competition only once and that was in December 2003. James Beattie scored both goals in a 2-0 win but the game is best – or worst – remembered for the visiting fans shamefully disrupting a minute's silence for Saints stalwart Ted Bates who had died a week earlier.

TED BATES TROPHY

In January 2004, Saints founded the Ted Bates Trophy as a tribute to their greatest servant who had died in November 2003. The first game was against Bayern Munich who attracted a capacity crowd for a friendly at St Mary's. The trophy was shared as Brett Ormerod's early goal was cancelled out by Michael Ballack in a 1-1 draw. The following pre-season saw Saints beat Italian side Chievo 3-1 with two goals by Kevin Phillips and one from Jelle Van Damme. A year later a Kenwyne Jones hat-trick gave Saints a thrilling 3-2 win over Champions League contenders Anderlecht. The trophy was shared again in 2006 when Saints drew 1-1 with Panathinaikos. David Prutton put the home side in front but the Greeks levelled 10 minutes from time. Saints suffered their first defeat as they were handed an Italian masterclass by Lazio who won 5-2 with plenty to spare. There was a huge gulf in class with Saints managing only two charitable penalties converted by Kenwyne Jones and Grzegorz Rasiak. The 2008 trophy was shared with West Ham who came from two down to draw 2-2 at St Mary's.

HOME FIRES BURNING

Saints were unbeaten at home throughout the whole of the 1921-22 season when they won the Third Division South title in only their second season in the Football League. They were also unbeaten in 10 league games from January 21 the previous season giving them a club record of 31 successive matches without defeat at The Dell. The run ended on August 28 when Leeds won 2-0 on the south coast.

TON UP

The most league goals Saints have scored in a season is 112 in 1957-58 when they finished sixth in Division Three (South). Two years later they won that division netting 106 goals in the process. In 1963-64 they bagged an exact century thanks to the six they got on the final day against Rotherham.

MEDAL COMES HOME

Saints splashed out more than £10,000 to keep Peter Rodrigues' FA Cup winners medal in the city. The unique piece of club memorabilia was put up for auction by Rodrigues' daughter who had been given it as a keepsake. The FA Cup-winning skipper unsuccessfully took legal action to try and prevent it going under the hammer and feared he would never see it again. It was sold for £10,200 to a mystery buyer, later revealed as Southampton Football Club who have displayed the medal at the stadium for all fans to enjoy.

TOP FEE?

There is now some debate about the highest transfer fee Saints have received. The top sale was defender Dean Richards who moved to Tottenham Hotspur for the fee of £8.1m in October 2001 but that was over-taken when striker Theo Walcott switched to Arsenal in January 2006. It was a complicated deal which saw Saints receive £5m immediately, a further £5m on club appearances, and potentially an extra £2m on international caps. But, the club's financial problems prompted them to call in the cash early in return for reduced terms. The settlement was kept confidential so the exact fee for Walcott remains unknown.

READER'S REWARD

Former Saints player George Reader took up the whistle when he finished playing and refereed the 1950 World Cup Final which saw Uruguay beat Brazil 2-1 in Rio di Janeiro. He went on to become a director and chairman of Southampton Football Club.

DEAN RICHARDS

ON THE RIGHT WAVELENGTH

Saints became the first club in the country to run its own FM radio station when they bought the franchise off South City in 2002. The Saint had already been running for more than year but it was restricted to the then-fledgling Sky digital, and the internet. However, the FM licence enabled it to expand its coverage of the club. It was sold to Town and Country Broadcasting in July 2007 and was re-named Radio Hampshire. It continued to broadcast from the specially equipped studios within the stadium.

ROCK ON

St Mary's staged its first ever rock concert in June 2005 when Elton John played a sell-out gig to an all-seated audience with Lulu as support act. A year later standing was introduced and Bon Jovi drew the biggest crowd yet for an event at St Mary's with a sell-out crowd of 35,000 packing the stadium. Supported by Nickelback, it was the fastest-selling date of the New Jersey rockers' UK *Have A Nice Day* tour. It was such a success that the band brought their *Lost Highway* tour to St Mary's in June 2008, attracting another huge crowd to confirm the stadium as one of the top concert venues in the south. The Dell never staged a rock concert although for many years it did play host to the Jehovah's Witnesses annual convention as a lucrative sideline. There was talk of a possible concert to mark the move to St Mary's with top Irish folk-rock band the Saw Doctors lined up to headline but in the end the club opted for a more sedate farewell dinner. Top impressionist Alistair McGowan provided the entertainment in a marquee erected on the pitch.

WORTH THE WAIT

Doug McGibbon had to wait six years between his away and home debuts! He made his first appearance for Saints in the 2-0 defeat at Plymouth in May 1939. However, the outbreak of war meant league football was suspended until September 1946 when McGibbon made his long-awaited home debut – and scored a hat-trick in the 4-0 win over Swansea in Division Two.

IF ANYONE CAN, MCCANN CAN

Neil McCann made history as he helped Scotland to a 3-1 win over the Faroe Islands. The left-winger became the first Southampton player ever to score for Scotland as he hit a dream volley after just eight minutes of the Euro 2004 qualifier. Only two Scottish Saints had previous played for their country while with the club, and both were one-cap wonders. Goalkeeper Ian Black played in a 2-0 defeat by England in April 1948, exactly 50 years after John Robertson also faced England. The half-back became the only outfield Saints player to represent Scotland until McCann pulled on the blue jersey. He won 10 of his 26 caps while with Southampton, the last of them against the United States alongside club colleague Nigel Quashie who won five caps while at St Mary's.

STATUE TED?

Ted Bates is widely regarded as the club's greatest servant so a group of fans put together a project to honour Mr Southampton with a statue outside the stadium. However, when it was unveiled in March 2007, the gasps were more in horror than admiration as the proportions and likeness were wrong. Described as a cross between comic Jimmy Krankie and former Pompey chairman Milan Mandaric, it was quickly removed and melted down. The Ted Bates Trust, though, worked tirelessly to put it right. Under the guidance of Dave Ford and personally funded for the most part by then club chairman Leon Crouch, the statue was re-commissioned. Renowned sculptor Sean Hedges-Quinn was brought in and with assistance from Stan Mitchell, he created a fitting tribute to the club's founding father. The statue now stands proudly at the front of the stadium.

SCOTT FREE

Young Aussie striker Scott McDonald made two Premiership appearances as substitute and one League Cup start but failed to make the grade for Saints. In March 2003 his contract was cancelled by manager Gordon Strachan who four years later spent £750,000 to buy him for Celtic from Motherwell.

MATT-TRICKS

Matthew Le Tissier's 209 goals for Saints included nine hat-tricks from his 462 appearances. The first came in a 4-0 win at home to Leicester on March 7, 1987 on a bitterly cold day with snow on the pitch. He swept home the first on 27 minutes from a Mark Wright knock-down and after Gordon Hobson had stretched the lead, the young Channel Islander sidefooted his second on 62 minutes. He then beat a string of defenders only to be denied by future team-mate Ian Andrews – before knocking in the rebound. Le Tissier had to wait almost three years for the next treble which came on February 27, 1990 in a 4-1 midweek win at home to Norwich. The Canaries took an early lead but were shot down by Le Tissier who levelled on 55 minutes, controlling neatly on a thigh before spinning to thump into the roof of the net. The second was special even by his standards and is included in his personal top ten. With deft close control and a clever drag-back, he turned Mark Bowen and former team-mate Andy Townsend inside out so they ended up colliding. Le Tissier then ran on to crack a low drive in off the base of a post. Kevin Moore got the third and then four minutes from time Francis Benali put Le Tissier away through the inside left channel. He spotted Bryan Gunn off his line and without breaking stride, chipped the keeper from 30 yards. After waiting three years for his second hat-trick, the third followed just three weeks later in a 3-3 draw at Wimbledon on March 17, 1990. The first goal saw his shot loop in off Eric Young but the Dons hit back to take a 3-1 lead, prompting Benali to see red with a horrendous tackle on John Fashanu who was launched so high in the air that he almost came down with snow on him! With 30 minutes on the clock, it looked a lost cause for the 10 men but just four minutes later Le Tissier controlled well to fire in from six yards. Another four minutes passed and the hat-trick was completed from the penalty spot – but that has faded in the memory compared to Benali's tackle which remains the major talking point from the day! The next treble took Saints to Wembley. It came in the second leg of the Zenith Data Systems Cup area-final against Chelsea in February 1992. Southampton were leading 2-0 from the home game and looked to have the tie sewn up after just six minutes of the return when Jason Cundy committed a professional foul on Alan Shearer to concede a penalty and pick up a red card. Dennis Wise tried to put off his former Dell colleague by betting him a sizeable sum he would miss. Inevitably, he lost. Le Tissier got his second on 20 minutes with a firm shot but 17 minutes later the Blues were handed a lifeline when the ball struck Neil Ruddock on the arm. Le Tissier went double or quits with Wise, who also scored from the spot. But Le Tissier booked Saints' first appearance at Wembley for 13 years when he ghosted behind the defence to control and fire home from close range on 51 minutes. Le Tissier's name still sends shivers through the fans of Oldham who were put through the wringer by the Saints star on the final day of the 1992-93 season. The Latics had to win and hope that Crystal Palace lost at Arsenal to survive. It soon became clear that the second part of the equation was a formality as the Eagles went down 3-0 at Highbury leaving Joe Royle's men needing only a win against a Saints side who were already safe. Neil Pointon's early goal was cancelled out by Le Tissier's low volley but the home crowd began to celebrate survival as goals by Ian Olney, Andy Ritchie and Gunnar Halle put them 4-1 up. However, on 67 minutes Le Tissier cracked in a 25-yard free-kick and he then headed in a Jeff Kenna cross with six minutes on the clock, plus interminable stoppage time. Joe Royle's men just held on to survive on goal difference, finishing just one place below Ian Branfoot's side. The arrival of Alan Ball as manager saw Le Tissier's career really take off and the mercurial striker marked his new mentor's first home game with another hat-trick. It came in the televised Valentine's Day massacre of Liverpool in 1994. Saints romped to a 4-2 win with the first goal taking just 28 seconds to arrive; a low 20-yard shot snaking past Bruce Grobbelaar on a snowy night. Craig Maskell got the second and Le Tissier converted two penalties on 43 and 49 minutes before the Merseysiders got two late consolations through a Julian Dicks penalty and Ian Rush. Despite that resurgence under Ball, Saints were still staring at relegation when they travelled to Norwich two months later on April 9. It was a game they had to win and their never-say-die spirit saw them home in a 5-4 thriller. Mark Robins' early goal was cancelled out by a Robert Ullathorne own goal just before half-time but it looked game over when Jeremy Goss and Chris Sutton scored quickfire goals after the break. Enter Matthew Le Tissier! The Saints legend saved his side with a classic hat-trick: left foot, right foot, header. The first was a low drive just inside a post from 18 yards on 57 minutes and the second a penalty just five minutes later. Typically, Saints pressed the self-destruct button and fell behind again within a minute to another Sutton goal. But on 72 minutes, Le Tissier nodded in from close range following a cross by Jeff Kenna and then the Channel Islander whipped in a corner for Ken Monkou to head a dramatic winner in injury-time. Le Tissier's biggest personal haul came in a Coca-Cola Cup second round tie at Huddersfield when he scored all the goals in a 4-0 win. He had also netted the only goal at The Dell in the first leg with a last-gasp header but he made sure there was no upset in the return opening the scoring with a spot-kick just before the break. He whipped in his second from the tightest of angles on 66 minutes and then three minutes later smacked home the rebound after Tommy Widdrington's shot had come back off a post. He grabbed his fourth six minutes from the end with a simple tap-in set up by Ronnie Ekelund. Three goals on the opening day of the 1995-96 season should have got Saints off to a flyer, but Le Tissier's treble counted for nothing as Nottingham Forest won 4-3 at The Dell. His 10th-minute penalty cancelled out Colin Cooper's thunderbolt two minutes earlier but Forest hit back through Ian Woan and Brian Roy. Another unerring penalty gave the home side hope but Roy restored the two-goal margin. Le Tissier curled in a 20-yard free-kick nine minutes from time but the visitors held firm. Le Tissier also got a hat-trick for the England B side in a 4-1 win against Russia at Loftus Road in April 1998. Billed as a final trial match for those hoping to break into Glenn Hoddle's World Cup squad, Le Tissier could not have done more. He scored three outstanding goals, made the other and hit the woodwork twice and yet he was inexplicably omitted from even the preliminary party for France 98.

DOUBLE TOP

Saints scooped the top two awards at the PFA dinner in 1982. Kevin Keegan was voted Player of the Year by his fellow professionals while Steve Moran was named Young Player of the Year. Matthew Le Tissier followed in Moran's footsteps in 1990, the same year former Southampton keeper Peter Shilton received his union's prestigious Merit Award.

BIZARRE INJURIES

Francis Benali tore a tendon in a hand while raking leaves in his garden to join a list of strange injuries suffered by players either before or during their time with the club. Charlie George cut off part of a finger with a lawn-mower while Dave Beasant was out for several weeks after dropping a jar of salad cream on a foot. And goalkeeper Michael Stensgaard somehow hurt himself with an ironing board!

CHAIRMEN – YEARS OF OFFICE

Dr E H Stancomb	1897-1909
T Chamberlayne	1909-1924
Col Wyndham Portal	1924-1929
Major R.C.H. Sloane Stanley	1929-1938
J R Sarjantson	1938-1943
A E Jakes	1943-1949
W Penn Barrow	1949-1951
J R Sarjantson	1951-1956
C J Cosgrove	1956-1961
J H G Barber	1961-1963
G Reader	1963-1978
A A Woodford	1978-1988
F G L Askham	1988-1997
R J G Lowe	1997-2006
M Wilde	2006-2007
L Crouch	2007-2008
M Wilde	2008-present

THE FLYING WAITER

Frankie Bennett worked part-time as a waiter while playing for Halesowen before his move to Saints in February 1993, following a successful short trial. He was brought in to provide decent service for Iain Dowie and was tipped for the top. But he never really got an extended run in the side, scoring just one league goal – a breakaway sprint in a 3-1 home win over Chelsea over Christmas 1993. He was eventually sold to Bristol Rovers for £50,000 in November 1996.

MOST CAPPED PLAYERS

Peter Shilton .... England 49 (125)
Chris Nicholl .... Northern Ireland 37 (51)
Neil McCann .... Scotland 10 (26)
Ron Davies............ Wales............................. 23 (37)
Tony Byrne............ Republic of Ireland....... 14 (14)

*
Bracketed figure shows total caps won

YOU CAN'T PARK HERE

For many years the club car park was patrolled by the legendary figure of Jack White who was harder to get past than the toughest centre-back. Even Kevin Keegan famously failed. He was due to provide match analysis for Sky when Saints hosted Manchester United in August 1992 – but he did not have a car park pass. The man who had once made the club the talking point of world football was refused entry and drove off in disgust leaving Sky to hastily commandeer the watching Ron Atkinson as their pundit. To make matters worse, United won 1-0 with a last-minute goal by Dion Dublin, the striker Ian Branfoot had wanted to sign. It was the first goal Saints had ever conceded in a live televised game

ANDY WILLIAMS RECORD

Andy Williams became the youngest Saints player to appear in a full international when he came off the bench for Wales in a friendly against Brazil in November 1999. That record was later over-taken by Gareth Bale who became Wales' youngest ever senior international at 16 years and 314 days when he played in a friendly against Trinidad and Tobago in May 2006. But it underlined the potential of Williams who made three Premiership starts and a further 18 appearances from the bench, using his pace on the left-wing against tiring defenders in the latter stages of games. However, he failed to push on and moved to Swindon for £60,000 in September 1999. Hernia problems affected his progress and he moved to Bath City before giving up the game to join the police.

DRAKE'S FORTUNE

Ted Drake became an Arsenal and England great, memorably netting all seven goals for the Gunners in their 7-1 thrashing of Aston Villa in December 1935. However, he owed much to the grounding he received at Southampton, who launched his career. Having missed a trial at Tottenham through injury, he worked as a gas-meter inspector and played part-time for Winchester City where he was spotted by Saints boss George Kay who signed him as an amateur in November 1931. The 19-year-old quickly made his mark, scoring five goals in 11 appearances during his debut season of 1931-32. The following campaign saw him net 20 in 33 to catch the eye of Arsenal. He travelled for talks but refused to sign and returned to The Dell to bang in 22 more goals in 27 Division Two games in 1933-34. This time a record fee of £6,000 was enough to lure him away and he became a Highbury legend before the war interrupted his career. His playing days were ended by a fall which damaged his back. A fine all-round sportsman, he also played county cricket for Hampshire from 1931-36. He managed Reading before taking over as Chelsea boss in 1952, guiding them to the League title in 1955. That earned him the distinction of becoming the first man to play in and manage a Championship-winning side.

BENEVOLENT GESTURE

Saints travelled to Oxford for a pre-season friendly in August 1996, competing for the Oxford Benevolent Cup. Despite a goal from Matthew Le Tissier, they were beaten 2-1 and the players duly trudged back to the dressing room while the home side collected a giant trophy. Further humiliation was unwittingly heaped on the Southampton players as organisers dragged them back out to receive runners-up medals!

RECORD DEFEAT REPEAT

Saints suffered their heaviest ever league defeat when they crashed 8-0 at Tottenham in Division Two on March 28, 1936 – and then matched it when they lost by the same score at Everton in Division One on November 20, 1971.

THE BOYS FROM BRAZIL

Brazil's dominance of world football can be blamed on Southampton – and one man in particular. Charles Miller is widely credited with introducing the game to the South American country. Although born in Brazil, he was educated in England at the request of his ex-pat father. He attended Bannisters School and played for Southampton St Mary's and Corinthians where he fell in love with the game. In 1894, the 19-year-old returned to his native Brazil disembarking in Santos – fittingly the Portuguese for Saints. He carried with him his boots and two footballs but was dismayed to find he had no-one to play with. The game was still unknown there so Miller decided to teach them. He marked out a pitch, gathered enough curious onlookers to form two teams and set up a game. The rest is history! Within 15 years, football was the biggest game in Brazil and Miller is still fondly remembered for it. He has a street named after him in Sao Paulo and one of their top teams was named Corinthians at his suggestion. His trick of flicking the ball up with his heel is still called a "Charleira".

HIGH FRY-ER

CB Fry remains one of the club's greatest ever sportsmen, even though he made just 16 Southern League appearances between 1900 and 1903. He would have made many more but was frequently unavailable due to his many other sporting commitments. Charles Burgess Fry equalled the world long jump record in 1893 and also went on to become one of the greatest England cricketers. He played for Corinthians until he joined Southampton in 1900 – but still insisted on wearing the striped socks of his former club in all games! He helped Saints to reach the FA Cup Final in 1902 and played in both the final and the replay against Sheffield United. He also represented England at football, winning his sole cap against Ireland at The Dell in March 1901. After finishing his football career, he played cricket for Sussex, Hampshire and England until 1921, scoring more than 30,000 first-class runs with an average of more than 50. He never lost a Test Match as captain and went on to have such a distinguished career as a teacher, politician, writer and publisher that the people of Albania offered him their throne!

ASSORTED RECORDS

Biggest Win

League	9-3 v Wolverhampton W	Sep 2 1965
	8-2 v Coventry City	Apr 1 1984
	6-0 v Wolverhampton W	Mar 31 2007
FA Cup	7-1 v Ipswich Town	Jan 3 1965
	6-0 v Luton Town	Feb 8 1995

Heaviest Defeat

League	0-8 v Tottenham Hotsput	Mar 2 1936
	0-8 v Everton	Nov 1 1971

Most Appearances

Terry Paine	809	1956-1974

Most Goals

Mike Channon	227	1966-1977, 1979-1982

Most Goals in a Season

Derek Reeves	44	1959-60

GARETH'S GOAL

Gareth Bale became the youngest player ever to score for Wales when he curled home a superb 25-yard free kick after 37 minutes of their crushing 5-1 home defeat by Slovakia on October 7, 2006.

POOR TURN-OUT

The lowest crowd for a league game at St Mary's was the 17,741 who witnessed the 1-0 win over relegation rivals Leicester in March 2008. Stern John's goal was enough for a first win under Nigel Pearson. The smallest for a competitive match at The Dell was just 1,875 for the 1-0 defeat to Port Vale in March 1936. Their smallest home gate in the Premier League was 9,028 for the visit of Ipswich in December 1993. Again Saints lost 1-0. The poor crowd was blamed on a fans' boycott in protest at manager Ian Branfoot who was sacked less than a month later.

PLAYER MANAGERS

Saints have never had a player-manager, although Dennis Wise was still registered as a midfielder when he jointly took caretaker charge with Dave Bassett for three games in December 2005. However, five players have gone on to manage the club since the war. Bill Dodgin signed as a centre-half in June 1939 and became manager in March 1946. Ted Bates became legendary arriving at the club in May 1937 and remaining there as player, coach, manager, chief executive, director and president until his death in November 2003. Alan Ball had two spells as a player from December 1976 to May 1978 and then from March 1981 to May 1982. He was manager from January 1994 to July the following year. He also managed Pompey, Stoke, Man City and Exeter. Chris Nicholl played for Saints from June 1977 to August 1983 and then returned to The Dell to succeed Lawrie McMenemy in August 1985. He went on to boss Walsall and the Northern Ireland under-21 side. Stuart Gray made 20 appearances between September 1991 and November 1993 and became the club's caretaker boss following the departure of Glenn Hoddle in March 2001. He was appointed full-time in June 2001 but sacked in November of the same year before taking over as boss of Northampton. Post-war Saints players who have gone on to manage other British league clubs include:

Micky Adams	Fulham, Swansea, Brentford
	Brighton, Leicester, Coventry
Alan Ball	Manchester City, Portsmouth, Exeter
Kevin Bond	Bournemouth
Jimmy Case	Brighton
Iain Dowie	Oldham, Crystal Palace Charlton, Coventry, QPR
Ted Drake	Reading, Chelsea
Ivan Golac	Torquay, Dundee Utd
Stuart Gray	Northampton
Mark Hughes	Wales, Blackburn, Man City
Joe Jordan	Bristol City, Hearts, Stoke, Bristol City
Kevin Keegan	Newcastle, Fulham, England, Man City
Alan Knill	Halifax, Rotherham
Sammy Lee	Bolton
Jim Magilton	Ipswich
John McGrath	Port Vale, Chester, Preston, Halifax

Jimmy Melia................. Aldershot, Southport, Brighton, Stockport
Mick Mills...Stoke, Colchester
Russell Osman.. Bristol City, Cardiff
Carlton Palmer... Stockport, Mansfield
Phil Parkinson ....Colchester, Hull City
Alf Ramsey.....................................Ipswich, England, Birmingham
Peter Reid... Sunderland, Leeds, Coventry
Dennis Rofe .... Bristol Rovers
Paul Tisdale .... Exeter
David Webb .... Bournemouth, Torquay, Southend
....Chelsea, Brentford
Dennis Wise...Millwall, Swindon, Leeds
Frank Worthington .... Tranmere
Mark Wright ....Oxford, Chester City, Peterborough

FASH BASH

In September 1982, Justin Fashanu became the first player to score for Saints while on loan from another club. He was brought in from Nottingham Forest where he was struggling to live up to his £1m price tag following a move from Norwich. Saints needed to beef up their front line following the shock departure of Kevin Keegan and the big striker settled well, netting the only goal in a 1-0 win at home to Aston Villa with a close-range volley. His impressive form worked against Lawrie McMenemy's men as it prompted Forest to recall him. His career was hampered by injury and personal problems which sadly led to him taking his own life in 1998.

TORPEDO'S AWAY

Uruguayan winger Federico Arias was known as the Torpedo, supposedly for his speed. It proved a fitting nickname as he sank without trace during a brief stay at the club.

CAPS FOR KEEPER

Peter Shilton won 49 of his 125 England caps while playing for Saints between 1982 and 1987, making him the club's most-capped player.

DIVISION ONE DEBUT

After a 46-year wait, Saints finally made their bow in the top-flight at home to Manchester City on August 20, 1966. A slightly disappointing crowd of just 19,900 turned out for the momentous occasion. Fittingly, their first ever goal in Division One was scored by Terry Paine who had netted their last in Division Two. He fired Southampton ahead on 42 minutes only for Mike Summerbee to earn the visitors a 1-1 draw with an equaliser 10 minutes into the second half.

UP THE MIDDLE FOR CHARLIE

That was the cry from fans who idolised Charlie Wayman, bought from Newcastle in 1947 for a then club-record fee of £10,000. Many of that generation still regard him as the club's finest forward and with 77 goals in 107 appearances, he still has the best goals-per-game ratio of any regular Southampton striker. He became an instant hit with 17 goals in 27 games which took Saints to within a whisker of promotion, finishing third in Division Two but four points behind his former club Newcastle. The following season saw Bill Dodgin's men go even closer. Again they finished third, just a point behind West Brom with Wayman netting 32 in 37 games – an astonishing return which included five in a 6-0 win at home to Leicester. He remains the only Saints player ever to score five in a league match. Fans would cry: "Up the middle for Charlie" and his intuitive positioning sense, pace, power and lethal left foot would normally do the rest. Older generations still wonder what might have been if Charlie had not torn a thigh muscle after scoring the winner at promotion rivals Spurs that season to put his side eight points clear at the top of the table. Saints won just one of their last seven to miss out by a point. The following season saw Wayman bag 24 goals in 36 games but once again Saints just missed out; this time on goal average behind both Sheffield clubs who were also on 52 points. However his wife was unable to settle in the south and he moved to Preston for £10,000 plus Eddy Brown. He did manage to help them to promotion and in 1954 he had the distinction of scoring in every round of the FA Cup including the final.

MATTY FOR ENGLAND

Sadly, Matthew Le Tissier joined the select band of supremely gifted players who did not win anywhere near as many caps as their talent deserved. The first of his eight full-international appearances came in a 1-0 friendly win against Denmark at Wembley on March 9, 1994. He came off the bench which meant frustratingly he was just beaten to an England debut by a Channel Island rival, Jersey's Graeme Le Saux started the match. Further substitute appearances followed in a 5-0 victory over Greece and a 0-0 draw with Norway before his first start for his country came with a 1-1 draw against Romania on October 12, 1994. He then came off the bench in a 1-0 win over Nigeria, all at Wembley. His second start and first away game was against the Republic of Ireland in Dublin on February 15, 1995. There had been a national clamour for the talented goalscorer to be given a proper chance by Terry Venables and many felt he had been set up to fail in a physical game in difficult conditions. England were trailing 1-0 when the game was abandoned because of crowd trouble midway through the first half and further credence was added to that conspiracy theory when Le Tissier did not even figure in the squad for the next match. He had to wait until September 1, 1996 for his next chance – and then it was only as a late substitute following scare stories that he might swap allegiance to France. All his previous internationals had been friendlies which would have allowed him to switch, although despite the French name, he was never eligible or inclined to play for anyone else. However, he came on in the 3-0 World Cup qualifier win against Moldova in Kishinev to tie him firmly to England. His third start and final cap came in the 1-0 home defeat by Italy at Wembley in a crucial World Cup group game. Le Tissier's brother Carl was wrongly blamed for leaking the line-up to the press, many of whom then unfairly singled out the Saints star as a scapegoat. Despite hitting a hat-trick in a 4-1 B international victory against Russia, Le Tissier was left out of even the preliminary squad for France 98 – even though the game had been billed as a trial.

TOP AWARD FOR CLAUS

Claus Lundekvam collected a giant trophy after winning the prestigious Norwegian PFA Footballer of the Year award in 2003.

TAKING A KNAPP

Ted Bates more than doubled Saints' record transfer outlay in August 1961 when he paid £27,500 and persuaded commanding centre-back Tony Knapp to drop down a division from FA Cup finalists Leicester. He added composure and class to the back line, helping them to eventual promotion to the top-flight in 1966. A year later he was recruited by Coventry for £20,000 after 260 appearances which brought two goals. He went on to have a hugely successful managerial career with Norwegian clubs Brann Bergen and Viking Stavanger among others – as well as with the Icelandic national side.

ENGLAND EXPECTS – EVENTUALLY

Saints have staged two full England internationals – 101 years apart. The first was in 1901 at the newly-built Dell, then one of the most modern grounds in the country. Goalkeeper Jack Robinson and CB Fry both represented Southampton as England beat Ireland 1-0. The club had to wait until October 16, 2002 for the chance to stage their second England game: a Euro Championship qualifier against Macedonia. With Wembley being rebuilt, the FA took the national side around the country and a capacity crowd of 32,095 saw a 2-2 draw with home defender Wayne Bridge starting the game. Sakiri gave the visitors a shock lead on 11 minutes only for David Beckham to level three minutes later. Trajanov restored the lead on 25 minutes but Steven Gerrard equalised on 36. Alan Smith was sent off in the closing stages.

ANIMAL MAGIC

If only Arsenal were nicknamed after bird or beast! When Saints reached the 2003 FA Cup final, there was a menagerie theme to their route. In the third round they were crowing over the cockerels of Tottenham with a 4-0 win at St Mary's and they followed that by taming the Lions at Millwall: 2-1 in a replay after a 1-1 draw. The Norwich Canaries were shot down 2-0 in the fifth round before Wolves were killed off by the same score in the quarter-final. That brought a semi-final against the Hornets of Watford and a 2-1 win put Saints into the final. There the animal magic ran out as they were gunned down 1-0 by the Arsenal.

BRETT ORMEROD IN ACTION IN THE 2003 FA CUP FINAL

TESTIMONIALS

Southampton, more than most, are a club who inspire loyalty so it is no surprise they have staged a succession of testimonials over the years. Luckiest recipient of all was Mike Channon whose game against QPR did not look, at first glance, to be anything out of the ordinary. But by a quirk of fate, the game was staged just two days after the team caused one of the great FA Cup Final shocks, beating Manchester United 1-0 at Wembley. Suddenly the whole city wanted to be inside The Dell to see the trophy paraded – and quite possibly they were! The official attendance was 29,508 but the turnstile counters surely packed up under the weight of what is generally thought to be the ground's biggest ever attendance. Fans picked out any possible vantage point from the roofs to the perimeter track. Thousands lined the actual pitch, getting in the way of the game which finished 2-2. Wembley hero Bobby Stokes again took centre stage with both goals against the side who were to finish runners-up to Liverpool that season. Fans were spilling onto the pitch long before the chaotic finish when a shot by Peter Osgood hit a spectator and flew in, sparking a mass pitch invasion not just from thousands inside the ground but also those previously locked out who spilled in through the exits. If that put the final score in some doubt, it was a trend which would be repeated when long-serving stalwarts Francis Benali and Matthew Le Tissier staged their testimonials. In May 1997, an ex-Saints side beat the Southampton first-team 8-7 – apparently! There was fun and farce in equal measure as previous and present players put on a pantomime which encapsulated the character of the club and of the beneficiary – who somehow popped in a genuine goal from 25 yards – and with his right foot! Dave Beasant played outfield, sticking the ball up his jumper and running the ball into the net from the halfway line, surrounded by a protective posse. And Le Tissier took his place in goal, defying Alan Shearer with a string of astonishing saves. Le Tissier's own benefit game was in a similar vein with a host of household names turning out as Saints took on an England XI. Le Tissier played 45 minutes for each and roped in his brothers and even his son Mitchell who scored four in a diplomatic 9-9 draw. At the final whistle, a montage of his best goals was played on the big screen to a sound track of My Way. Le Tissier summed up the mood of the night telling the crowd: "I did it My Way – but I like to think I also did it Your Way!" The most recent recipient is Claus Lundekvam who welcomed Celtic to St Mary's in July 2008 after his 12 years with the club were ended by an ankle injury. Two managers have received testimonials. Leeds were the visitors for Ted Bates' richly-deserved game in August 1974, a 1-1 draw. However Pompey were initially advertised as the opponents with the game scheduled for four months earlier. But with Saints heading for relegation, the game was wisely called off. Lawrie McMenemy's achievements were rewarded in May 1979, Nottingham Forest won 4-0 in front of a slightly disappointing turn-out of 14,693.

Post-war testimonials

Ron Reynolds v Chelsea	Apr 29 1964	won 3-2
John Hollowbread v Portsmouth	May 10 1966	won 6-1
Tommy Traynor v Twente Enschede	Oct 31 1966	drew 3-3
John Sydenham v Portsmouth	Apr 20 1970	lost 2-4
Ted Bates v Leeds United	Aug 14 1974	drew 1-1
Terry Paine v Ipswich Town	Apr 29 1975	drew 1-1
Mike Channon v QPR	May 3 1976	drew 2-2
Lawrie McMenemy v N Forest	May 11 1974	lost 0-4
George Horsfall v Glasgow Rangers	May 16 1982	won 4-2
Nick Holmes v Benfica	Aug 5 1986	won 4-1
Francis Benali v Ex-Saints	May 13 1997	lost 7-8
Jason Dodd v Woggy's Wanderers	May 22 2001	lost 1-3
Matthew Le Tissier v England XI	May 14 2002	drew 9-9
Danny Wallace v All Stars	May 17 2004	drew 2-2
Claus Lundekvam v Celtic	July 18 2008	lost 0-2

COCA-COLA KID

When Saints paid Manchester City £750,000 for Bradley Wright-Phillips in July 2006, a third of the fee was paid by Coca-Cola. Southampton won top prize of £250,000 in a promotion by the Football League sponsors with the cash to be used to buy or put towards a player. The club used the welcome cash to buy Wright-Phillips who scored on his debut after coming on as substitute in a 2-2 draw at Derby.

THE GOAL THAT NEVER WAS

Saints went down 3-0 to a Michael Bridges hat-trick as Leeds won 3-0 at The Dell in August 1999. But it might have been so much different if an "equaliser" had counted. Mark Hughes struck an edge-of-the-area shot with such venom that the ball flew back out of the net, apparently after hitting a stanchion at the back of the goal. It happened so quickly that the referee did not realise that the ball had gone in and waved play on.

TV HIGHLIGHT

The first live BBC televised game at The Dell was the 2-0 win over Liverpool on Friday March 16, 1984. Both goals came from Danny Wallace, the first was the goal of the season to wow the watching audience. Mark Wright played the ball out of defence for Frank Worthington whose 40-yard pass picked out Mark Dennis. His cross was nodded back at the far post for Wallace to score a spectacular goal with an acrobatic scissor kick.

ROFE JUSTICE

Dennis Rofe has been sacked three times by Saints. The former England under-23 left-back signed for Southampton from Chelsea in July 1982. He made 20 first-team appearances before joining the coaching staff in July 1984. He was Chris Nicholl's right-hand man until the manager was sacked in May 1991. Somewhat harshly, Rofe went too. Saints had assumed the new boss would want his own man alongside him but that was not the case. After a successful spell as caretaker boss, Rofe became Bristol Rovers manager in December 1991 but returned to The Dell in July 1995 when he was appointed as youth team coach by Dave Merrington. Sacked a year later by Graeme Souness, Rofe returned for a third spell in April 1998. He was appointed as Academy coach and then moved up to the Reserves the following November before regaining his position as first-team coach under Stuart Gray in March 2001. He was sacked again in December 2005 following the appointment of George Burley who discarded most of the coaching staff.

HOUSE FULL

When Saints hosted Chelsea for their first league game at St Mary's in August 2001, they drew their biggest attendance for more than 24 years. It was their largest home crowd since the FA Cup fifth round tie against Manchester United in February 1977 when 29,137 fans paid then record receipts of £39,200! It was the last time The Dell was to house more than 29,000. The tie – a re-run of the previous season's final – finished in a 2-2 draw with David Peach and Nick Holmes scoring for Saints. United won the replay and went on to win the final.

ELECTRICAL LEEDS

Saints took more than two and a half hours to complete their League Cup tie against Leeds on December 5, 1960 – and they did not even have extra-time! It was one of the most remarkable games ever seen at The Dell – or rather not seen as a floodlight failure twice plunged the ground into darkness. **7.30pm**: Kick-off. **7.40pm**: First floodlight failure. **7.57pm**: Players return to dressing rooms after being told that electricians are working to repair the fault. **8.09pm**: Game resumes with lights at two-thirds power. **8.15pm**: Derek Reeves heads Saints in front from a Terry Paine cross. **8.20pm**: Saints keeper Ron Reynolds is hurt. As he is being treated, the lights go out again. He is stretchered off in pitch darkness. **8.54pm**: The lights come back on with full power to reveal Cliff Huxford in goal in place of Reynolds and Southampton down to 10 men with substitutes yet to be invented. **8.57pm**: Reeves makes it 2-0 from another Paine pass. **9.05pm**: Paine again sets up Reeves who completes his hat-trick from close range. **9.17pm**: Half-time Saints lead 3-0. **9.25pm**: Second half starts with Leeds now also down to 10 men through injury. **9.28pm**: Reeves gets his fourth and Paine again is the provider. **9.32pm**: Peyton scores what looks to be merely a consolation. **9.42pm**: McCole gets a second for Leeds. **9.48pm**: Suddenly nerves are jangling as Jack Charlton pulls it back to 4-3. **9.58pm**: Huge drama as Cameron nets a penalty to make it 4-4. **10.09pm**: With just seconds remaining, Reeves sensationally scores his fifth to win it for Saints. **10.10pm**: Full-time Saints win an astonishing game 5-4!

GOALSCORING DUO

Exactly 800 games between them and only three goals! Claus Lundekvam netted just two goals in 411 appearances for Saints; while Francis Benali managed just one in 389 games. Yet both began their careers as strikers! Lundekvam was a prolific marksman for his school and youth teams while growing up in Norway while Benali played centre-forward for England Schools at Wembley!

BARN CHANCES

Saints fans have enjoyed some barn-storming performances when their side have come up against Barnsley in recent years. The 2-2 draw at Oakwell on December 29, 2007 made it a total of 32 goals in the last six meetings between the clubs. The Tykes' only season in the Premiership brought a 4-1 defeat at The Dell in November 1997 although they won the return 4-3 in March 1998. The next meeting was in the Championship in August 2006 when the sides drew 2-2 at Oakwell with Saints winning 5-2 at St Mary's in the following February. The South Yorkshire side gained a dramatic last-gasp 3-2 win on the south coast in September 2007 before squandering a two-goal lead in the wind and rain at Oakwell.

STORMIN' NORMAN

Norman Dean is the last Saints player to score a hat-trick against local rivals Pompey. It came during the promotion season 1965-66 and proved crucial as it helped his side to a 5-2 win at Fratton Park. Dean and Martin Chivers put the visitors 2-0 up in 23 minutes but the home side drew level just before the hour. However Dean netted twice more with Chivers rounding off the scoring. Those goals were the highlight of his time at The Dell. He came on trial and then signed amateur forms while he completed a welding apprenticeship, signing professional in April 1963. He scored a total of 11 goals in 20 appearances before moving to Cardiff for £6,000 in March 1967. He moved to Barnsley 17 months later but a broken leg effectively ended his career and he now works as a security officer at the Saints training ground in Marchwood.

PENALTY KING

Matthew Le Tissier is the undisputed king of the penalty kick, failing just once in 48 attempts from the spot. Inevitably, the only blemish came from a save rather than missing the target, something which the set-piece specialist regards as a cardinal sin with a free shot from 12 yards. The man with the unique distinction of stopping a Le Tissier penalty is Mark Crossley who dived to his right to save as Nottingham Forest won 2-1 at The Dell on March 24, 1993. The Saints star did have some measure of consolation by scoring with a terrific 25-yard volley but it was not enough to earn his side a point. Le Tissier also went on to beat Crossley with three more penalties in future games. Le Tissier began taking penalties almost by accident. Neil Ruddock and Paul Rideout had both missed so a training ground competition was set up to decide their successor. Le Tissier won and began an unparalleled run of success from the spot converting 47 out of 48, beginning with one in a 2-2 draw at home to Wimbledon in September 1989.

Le Tissier's penalty record
1989-90

Sept 30	Wimbledon (h)	2-2
Oct 14	QPR (a)	4-1
Nov 18	Chelsea (a)	2-2
Dec 2	Millwall (a)	2-2
Dec 30	Sheffield Wednesday (h)	2-2
Jan 24	Oldham Athletic (Lge Cup) (h)	2-2
Mar 17	Wimbledon (a)	3-3
Apr 28	Coventry City (h)	3-0

1990-91

Nov 3	Wimbledon (a)	1-1
Feb 23	QPR (a)	1-2
Mar 23	Chelsea (a)	2-0
Apr 13	Sunderland (h)	3-1
May 4	Derby County (a)	2-6

1991-92

Sep 4	a	1-2
Oct 26	Nottingham Forest (a)	3-1
Jan 7	West Ham United (ZDS Cup) (h)	2-1

Jan 29...Chelsea (ZDS Cup) (a) 3-1
1992-93
Aug 29...Middlesbrough (h) 2-1
Oct 7 ....Gillingham (Lge Cup) (h) 3-0
Mar 13...Ipswich Town (h) 4-3
Mar 24...................................... Nottingham Forest (miss) (h) 1-2
1993-94
Jan 15... Coventry City (h) 1-0
Feb 14.................................... Liverpool (two pens) (h) 4-2
Apr 9 ....Norwich City (a) 5-4
Apr 16 .... Blackburn Rovers (h) 3-1
May 7 .... West Ham United (a) 3-3
1994-95
Sep 12....................................Tottenham Hotspur (a) 2-1
Sep 17....................................Nottingham Forest (h) 1-1
Oct 5 ....Huddersfield Town (Lge Cup) (h) 4-0
Nov 2.. Norwich City (h) 1-1
Jan 2 ....Sheffield Wednesday (a) 1-1
Feb 8....................................Luton Town (FA Cup) (h) 6-0
Feb 18................................ Tottenham Hotspur (FA Cup) (a) 1-1
Mar 1....................................Tottenham Hotspur (FA Cup) (h) 2-6
1995-96
Aug 18...................... Nottingham Forest (h) 3-4 (two pens)
Apr 6 .... Blackburn Rovers (h) 1-0
1996-97
Aug 21... Leicester City (a) 1-2
Oct 19..Sunderland (h) 3-0
Nov 2....................................Sheffield Wednesday (a) 1-1
Feb 22...................................... Sheffield Wednesday (h) 2-3
1997-98
Nov 8..Barnsley (h) 4-1
Feb 18.. Coventry City (h) 1-2
Mar 7..Everton (h) 2-1
Mar 28...................................... Newcastle United (h) 2-1
1998-99
Aug 29....................................Nottingham Forest (h) 1-2
1999-00
April 1 ....Sunderland (h) 1-2

TIMELY TERRY

Terry Curran scored just one goal for Saints – but it could hardly have been more important. His solitary strike for the club was enough to put them in the 1979 League Cup final. Lawrie McMenemy's men had fought back from two down to draw 2-2 at Leeds in the first leg of the semi-final with goals by Nick Holmes and Steve Williams cancelling out a fine curler by Tony Currie and an effort from Ray Hankin. After 11 minutes of the second leg, Curran lashed the ball into the roof of the net and Saints hung on to win 1-0 and 3-2 on aggregate, earning their third Wembley appearance in as many years. They eventually lost 3-2 to Nottingham Forest despite goals by David Peach and Nick Holmes. Little over a week later, Curran moved on to Sheffield Wednesday for £100,000 – £40,000 more than Saints had paid to Derby just seven months earlier.

THIRD TIME LUCKY

The last time Saints went to a second replay in the FA Cup was in the third round of the competition in 1978. After a 0-0 draw away and again at home to Fourth Division Grimsby, second-tier Saints went to a third game against the Mariners at a neutral venue, Leicester's Filbert Street. This time they made no mistake winning 4-1 with goals by David Peach, Phil Boyer, Ted MacDougall and Nick Holmes. Second replays were scrapped in the 1991-92 season in favour of penalty shoot-outs with Saints beneficiaries as they beat Manchester United at Old Trafford for the first time in the FA Cup, winning the shoot-out 4-2.

ALL-TIME TOP LEAGUE GOAL SCORERS

185	Mike Channon	1966-77 and 1979-82
161	Matthew Le Tissier	1986-2002
160	Terry Paine	1956-74
156	Bill Rawlings	1920-27
154	George O'Brien	1959-66
145	Derek Reeves	1955-62
145	Eric Day	1945-57
134	Ron Davies	1966-73

FA CUP FINAL: FAMOUS FOUR – 1900 & 1902

Saints have reached the FA Cup Final four times in their history – playing two finals and one replay at Crystal Palace, once at Wembley Stadium and the fourth final at the Millennium Stadium, Cardiff, while the national stadium was being redeveloped. The first occasion was in 1900, two years after losing the semi-final 2-0 to Nottingham Forest in a replay at Crystal Palace following a 1-1 draw at Bramall Lane. That defeat still rankled and helped spur them on to become the first ever Southern League side to reach the final of the competition. Having won the title three years in succession, Southampton switched their focus to the FA Cup and so only finished third in the Southern League. They began by beating Everton 3-0 in the first round and followed that up with a 4-1 win at home to Newcastle – helped by a timely abandonment. They had lost star striker Jack Farrell with a dislocated collar bone and with substitutes not even imagined at that time, they were up against it. But a snowstorm forced the game to be called off and when it was staged again the following week, Saints won 4-1. The following week, West Brom were dispatched 2-1 to earn a semi-final against Millwall at Crystal Palace. It finished 0-0 but Southampton won the replay 3-0 at Elm Park to reach their first major final just 15 years after their formation. Amid rumours of an Anglo-Scottish split in the camp, Southampton failed to produce their best form and lost 4-0 to Bury with three of the goals coming in the first 20 minutes, to the disappointment of the 4,000 Saints fans who made their way to Crystal Palace. The following season they lost 3-1 at home to Everton in the first round but the club returned to the showpiece at Crystal Palace in 1902 and this time gave a much better account of themselves, losing to Sheffield United, only after a replay. The campaign began with a 2-1 win over Southern League rivals Tottenham in a second replay at Reading's Elm Park after a 1-1 draw away and a 2-2 score at home. A 4-1 win at Liverpool was followed by 3-2 revenge against Bury before beating Nottingham Forest 3-1 at White Hart Lane in the semi-finals. In front of almost 75,000 people, they drew 1-1 with the previous year's beaten finalists Sheffield United only to lose the replay 2-1.

FARMER JONES

There was no danger of goalkeeper Paul Jones ever taking the good life for granted. Before breaking into the professional ranks late with Wolves in 1991, he used to be a dairy farmer. Regularly starting his long days before six o'clock in the morning, the down-to-earth Welsh international was well aware of how most fans work for a living. However, he was far from the only recent Southampton player to have had another profession before making it in football. Utility player Jo Tessem was a policeman in Norway before joining Lyn Oslo in 1996. He then moved to Molde where he sufficiently impressed in a pre-season friendly against Southampton for Dave Jones to sign him. Frankie Bennett became known as the Flying Waiter because he served diners in a Birmingham hotel while playing part-time for Halesowen Town before signing for Saints in 1993. Jon Gittens was a tailor playing for Paget Rangers when Chris Nicholl signed him in 1985. He exercised his freedom of contract to sign for Swindon in July 1987 with the tribunal setting the fee at a paltry £40,000. Nicholl bought him back for 10 times that fee in March 1991. Midfielder Jimmy Case was a trained electrician before embarking on a glittering career with Liverpool in 1973. He moved to Brighton in 1981 and then Southampton in March 1985 as Lawrie McMenemy's last signing for the club. Case was supposed to be a stop-gap for a season or so – but stayed for six years, producing some of the best football of his career. Even after hanging up his boots, he still used his qualifications occasionally acting as a roadie for top group Echo and the Bunnymen. Former striker Iain Dowie was known as the Rocket Man after working with British Aerospace and former winger Keith Cassells had a job as a postman before stamping his mark on football with some quality deliveries from the wing. After hanging up his boots, he became a policeman. Midfielder Andy Townsend was a computer operator for Greenwich Borough Council while playing for Weymouth before Saints spotted him in 1985. He was recommended by the club's then commercial manager Bob Russell and stayed at The Dell until August 1988 when he signed for Norwich for 10 times the initial £35,000 outlay. He went on to star for Chelsea, Aston Villa and Middlesbrough before becoming a respected pundit for ITV.

FA CUP FINAL: FAMOUS FOUR: 1976

After reaching the FA Cup Final twice in three seasons, Saints had to wait 74 years for their next chance of glory – and this time they took it with an unforgettable victory over Manchester United. The club's greatest triumph almost ended as soon as it began. Lawrie McMenemy's Second Division side were trailing 1-0 at home to Aston Villa when Hughie Fisher grabbed a dramatic injury-time equaliser which was to take on huge significance. Saints won the replay 2-1 after extra-time with both goals coming from Jim McCalliog and they followed it up with a comfortable 3-1 success over Second Division rivals Blackpool. They won with two goals from Mike Channon and one from Bobby Stokes who netted again in the fifth round to earn a 1-1 draw at West Brom, another Second Division side. Channon hit a hat-trick as Saints won the replay 4-0 to reach the quarter-finals for the first time since 1963. They began to wonder if their name might be on the cup as their luck of the draw held again with a visit to Fourth Division Bradford City. The Yorkshire side attempted to cash in on their big day and tripled seat prices. They also raised the cost of a terrace ticket from the normal 65p to £1.50! Saints complained to the FA who backed the Bantams but the home club got what they deserved as their attendance of 14,194 was around 9,000 below their capacity. It was also, by 8,000, the smallest gate for an FA Cup sixth round tie since the war. Further punishment was exacted as Saints won 1-0 with a spectacular 20-yard free-kick. Peter Osgood flipped the ball up to McCalliog who scored with a volley past the stunned keeper. Again Saints' luck held in the draw where they could have met the teams who were destined to finish third and fourth in the First Division – or Third Division Crystal Palace. The first name drawn from the hat was Derby, then a real force. The tension mounted until the announcer uttered the wonderful words "will play Manchester United or Wolverhampton Wanderers" – thus depriving neutrals of the final most of the country wanted to see. Indeed, United boss Tommy Docherty lived to regret calling his side's semi "the real final". Having lost their two previous finals at Crystal Palace, Saints now faced them for a place at Wembley – and they duly won the clash at Stamford Bridge 2-0. Paul Gilchrist put them in front with a 25-yard shot on 74 minutes and the tie was won from the penalty spot five minutes later after Channon had been brought down. There was a strong suspicion it might have been outside the area and television appeared to confirm that – but again Southampton's luck held and David Peach took the first of his 24 penalties for the club to secure a place at Wembley. United were hot favourites to win but the Southampton side was packed with experience and know-how and, led shrewdly by McMenemy, who played on the underdog status and heaped all the pressure on the favourites who were not allowed to play. United had plenty of pressure but rarely hurt Saints who snatched a stunning 1-0 victory seven minutes from time. Ian Turner's long kick was laid off by Channon for McCalliog to chip through for Bobby Stokes. He let the ball bounce and brushed a 20-yard shot past Alex Stepney into the bottom right corner. The offside flag stayed down and although debates were to rage long and hard for years afterwards, the goal stood and Southampton had won the FA Cup.

TEXACO CUP

In 1974 Saints were invited to take part in the Texaco Cup, a prestigious Anglo-Scottish competition. Their pre-season group games saw them draw 1-1 at Luton then beat Orient 2-1 and West Ham 2-0 at The Dell. That earned a quarter-final against mighty Glasgow Rangers. Southampton won 3-1 away with two goals from Peter Osgood and one from George O'Brien. They finished the job at home with a 2-0 victory courtesy of Paul Gilchrist and an own goal. The semi-final brought an almost identical outcome, this time against Oldham. Again Southampton won 3-1 away this time with two from Mike Channon and one from Mel Blyth. The home leg produced a 2-1 success with goals by Channon and Bobby Stokes. Channon scored the only goal of the home leg of the final against Newcastle as Saints secured a slender 1-0 lead. John Tudor netted 13 minutes from the end of the second leg to take it to extra-time. Nine minutes into the additional half hour, Jim Steele was sent off and it hit Saints hard. The 10 men conceded goals to Tudor and Cannell to go down 3-0 on the night and 3-1 on aggregate.

FA CUP FINAL: FAMOUS FOUR – 2003

It took 27 years and two semi-final disappointments in 1984 and 1986 before Saints again reached the final in 2003. Once again they had the luck of the draw. Just as they had done in 1976, they played top-flight opposition in the third round and then not again until the final. They began at home to a disinterested Tottenham side who looked deflated by their 1-0 Premiership defeat at St Mary's just three days previously. Saints turned on a treat for the television cameras and won 4-0 with goals by Michael and Anders Svensson, Jo Tessem and James Beattie. Just as they had done in 1976, Saints needed a last-minute reprieve to stay in the competition, this time in the fourth round at home to Division One side Millwall. Those looking for omens could take heart from the fact that Southampton had never lost to the Lions in their four previous meetings in the competition, and each time had gone on to reach at least the semi-final. However, the underdogs led through former Pompey striker Steve Claridge who had earlier been denied by a sliding goal-line clearance from recalled stalwart Francis Benali. In the closing minutes Kevin Davies salvaged a draw and Saints won the replay 2-1 in extra-time, both goals coming from Matt Oakley to set up a home tie against Norwich. Saints won 2-0 with goals by Anders Svensson and Tessem and triumphed by the same score in the quarter-final at home to Wolves thanks to Chris Marsden and a Paul Butler own goal. The semi-finals consisted of mighty Arsenal (or Chelsea) – and three clubs wanting to avoid them! Two were from the second tier, and Saints got the tie they would probably have chosen, facing Watford, bizarrely at Villa Park rather than in north London. By the time they kicked off, Saints knew they were playing for a place in Europe. Arsenal had already won the first semi-final and as they were guaranteed a Champions League spot, the competition's UEFA Cup slot would go to the runners-up. Watford had yet to concede a goal on their cup run but Brett Ormerod breached their defence three minutes before half-time with his first goal since October as he headed in a Chris Marsden cross. With 11 minutes on the clock, James Beattie hustled Robinson into diverting Ormerod's low cross into his own net. There was a nervy finale as Marcus Gayle headed in three minutes from time but Gordon

Strachan's side held on for a 2-1 win and a guaranteed place in Europe as well as the FA Cup final. No-one fortunate enough to have been at the Millennium Stadium will ever forget the wall of yellow created by the Saints supporters who outnumbered and out-sang their Arsenal counterparts to create an amazing atmosphere. With the roof closed on a miserable morning, Saints walked out to a tumultuous roar with their line-up containing 21-year-old Chris Baird who was making only his second senior start for the club. Sadly, Saints went down 1-0 to a goal by their perennial tormentor Robert Pires just before half-time. James Beattie had an effort disallowed for a tight offside and Brett Ormerod was denied late on by a stunning save from David Seaman on his farewell appearance for the Gunners. But Saints, who lost goalkeeper Antti Niemi with a calf strain, could not quite find the goal which would have raised the roof!

CHANGING JANES

A player called Janes scored a hat-trick as Maidenhead pulled off a stunning 4-0 win over Southampton St Mary's at the Antelope Ground in the 1892-93 FA Cup campaign. Apart from a charity cup final defeat by Royal Engineers, it was the first cup-tie the club had ever lost and it prompted them to sign Janes. They made him their first official professional player – although Hagiology historians would later discover that the club had actually paid £1 a week to Jack Dollin but had kept it a secret! Janes never played for Southampton as the FA ordered him to return to Maidenhead after upholding his former club's complaint that Janes was in no fit condition to know what he was doing when he signed for the Saints!

IS THAT IT?

The briefest ever Saints first-team career was that of Cedric Baseya who came on as a substitute in the 1-1 draw at home to Ipswich on March 1, 2008. The final whistle sounded just 30 seconds later before he had even touched the ball. He exercised his freedom of contract and left the club for Lille in June of the same year and without another senior appearance.

MILLION MAN

The first time Saints splashed out a seven-figure sum on a player was in December 1990 when Chris Nicholl broke the club transfer record to sign Alan McLoughlin from Swindon for £1m. McLoughlin had scored a stunning goal in a League Cup tie against Saints 11 months earlier and his call-up to the Irish World Cup squad for Italia 90 sealed his switch. He was most effective playing just behind the front two but was often used out of position on the left and so struggled to show his best form, moving to Pompey in March 1992 after netting just one goal in 27 appearances.

DEREK DOMINATES

Saints' top league goalscorer in one season is Derek Reeves who hit 44 in 1959-60. Five of those came in a 5-4 League Cup win over Leeds at The Dell. That equalled the most goals scored by a Saints player in one post-war match. Charlie Wayman also netted five in a Division Two 6-0 win against Leicester in October 1948. The most goals ever scored in one game by a Saints player was Albert Brown who banged in seven in an 11-0 win over Northampton in a Southern League fixture in December 1901.

YOUNG GUNS

Saints have always had a strong youth policy bringing through such home-grown stars as Mike Channon and Terry Paine right through the likes of Alan Shearer, the Wallaces and Matthew Le Tissier to more recent stars such as Theo Walcott, Gareth Bale and Andrew Surman. But it was not until 2005 that they reached the final of the FA Youth Cup for the first time. They drew 2-2 against Ipswich Town at St Mary's only to lose the second leg 1-0 to a goal late in extra-time. Under the guidance of Georges Prost they also reached the semi-final the following year, losing only on penalties to the eventual winners Liverpool. During his six years at the club, the French coach guided the Southampton Under 18s to the FA Premier League Academy title in 2006 and to runners-up spot two years earlier. They also won their divisional title in each of his six seasons in charge.

SAINTS MANAGERS

Between 1955 and 1985 Saints had just two managers, a period of stability which brought huge success. Ted Bates took the club from the third tier to the top-flight during his reign from 1955 until 1973 when he handed over to Lawrie McMenemy for the club's golden era. He was a hard act to follow but Chris Nicholl survived for six seasons before becoming the first manager ever to be sacked by Saints, who have since made up for lost time since! McMenemy's appointment began a trend where each successive manager would stay around half as long as his predecessor. Bates was in charge for 28 years, McMenemy for 12, Chris Nicholl for six, Ian Branfoot for almost three, Alan Ball for 18 months and Dave Merrington for 10 months before he was sacked in 1996. Since then Saints – once known for their stability – have had 11 permanent managers in 12 years. Graeme Souness had one season before quitting to be replaced by Dave Jones whose stint was prematurely ended by totally unfounded allegations of child abuse. He was given gardening leave to prepare his defence which was not needed as the case collapsed almost as soon as it began with the judge decreeing it should never have got to court. Glenn Hoddle took over for a year before returning to his "spiritual home" of Tottenham. After a brief stint as caretaker boss, Stuart Gray was given the job full-time in June 2001 but was sacked the following October after a patchy start to the campaign. His replacement was Gordon Strachan who was not initially well received by the fans but they quickly came to love the Ginger Genius as he led them to the FA Cup final. In January 2004, he announced his intention not to renew his contract at the end of the season as he needed a break and that effectively forced Saints to replace him sooner. Steve Wigley took over as caretaker while chairman Rupert Lowe debated whether to bring back Hoddle amid protests from the fans angry at the way he had left the club previously. Instead, in March 2004 he opted for Paul Sturrock who lasted only two games into the next season before leaving by mutual consent. Wigley again took charge until December of the same year when he was replaced by Harry Redknapp. The former Pompey boss failed to save Saints from relegation and returned to his "spiritual home" in December 2005. Dave Bassett and Dennis Wise took temporary charge before George Burley was appointed just before Christmas 2005. He stayed just over two years but left the club in January 2008 to become manager of Scotland. John Gorman and Jason Dodd were named as caretaker managers but patchy results saw Nigel Pearson brought in. Again, he was not initially a popular appointment but he soon won over the fans with his honesty, passion and tactical awareness. He kept the team up on the final day of the campaign but his contract was not renewed in June 2008 when Dutch duo Jan Poortvliet and Mark Wotte took charge.

1894-95 .... Cecil Knight (secretary/manager)
1895-97 .... Charles Robson
1897-1911 .... E Arnfield
1911-12 ....George Swift
1912-24 ....Jimmy McIntyre
1925-31 .... Arthur Chadwick
1931-36 ....George Kay
1936-37 ....George Gross
1937-43 .... Tom Parker
1943-46 .... Arthur Dominy
1946-49 .... Bill Dodgin Snr
1949-51 ....Sid Cann
1952-55 ....George Roughton
1955-73 .... Ted Bates
1973-85 .... Lawrie McMenemy
1985-91 .... Chris Nicholl
1991-94 ....Ian Branfoot
1994-95 .... Alan Ball
1995-96 ....Dave Merrington
1996-97 .... Graeme Souness
1997-2000 .... Dave Jones
2000-01 .... Glenn Hoddle
2001 .... Stuart Gray
2001-04 ....Gordon Strachan
2004 .... Paul Sturrock
2004 ....Steve Wigley
2004-05 ....Harry Redknapp
2005-08 ....George Burley
2008 ....Nigel Pearson
2008- ....Jan Poortvliet

WISE DECISION

In November 1975, midfielder Bobby Stokes was given the chance of a transfer to his home-town club Portsmouth in exchange for Paul Went but he turned it down saying he did not feel it was the right move for him. Six months later he scored the most important goal of his career to win the FA Cup for Southampton.

PEACH OF A PLAYER

When David Peach converted a penalty against Manchester United on August 18, 1979 he became the highest scoring full-back in the Football League's history. In total he netted 44 goals in 278 appearances, becoming something of a spot-kick specialist which saw him miss just one out of 24 attempts. Memorably, the first came in the 1976 FA Cup semi-final. Mike Channon had missed two in a row so Peach – Lawrie McMenemy's first signing for the club at a bargain £50,000 from Gillingham – was detailed to take over. He was desperately hoping it would not happen in such a big game and when the chance came he gambled that the keeper would dive one way or the other. He hit it down the middle, later describing it as his worst-ever penalty but it was enough to take Saints to Wembley. Along with Nick Holmes, he is one of only two men to have played twice at Wembley for Saints and he was included on England's tour of South America in 1977 but failed to get a game to add to his under-21 caps. It was something of a surprise when he was transferred to Swindon for £150,000 in March 1980. There he achieved the distinction of becoming the only player in the League to have played on every ground.

BOG-EY MAN

Thomas Bogan made the briefest international appearance of all-time in a war-time match against England at Hampden in April 1945. In the very first minute he tumbled over England keeper Frank Swift and twisted his knee so badly that he had to go off. The striker, who went on to score two goals in nine Southampton appearances between December 1951 and August 1953, never pulled on a Scotland shirt again.

RETURN OF THE MAC

Lawrie McMenemy has had three spells with Saints in various roles. Although he never played league football, he was a shrewd operator as a manager and brought unprecedented success to the club. A former guardsman, the giant Geordie made his name in the game with Doncaster and Grimsby before taking over as manager from Ted Bates in November 1973. He was grateful for the club's policy at the time of standing by their managers and giving them a chance to build as Saints were relegated that season – the first victims of the new three up, three down system. He set about rebuilding and led the club to their greatest ever moment, and sole piece of major silverware, as his Second Division underdogs beat mighty Manchester United 1-0 at Wembley in the 1976 FA Cup final. Two years later he led Southampton to promotion then to a League Cup final, into Europe and to runners-up spot in Division One. The charismatic boss did it with an exciting brand of attacking football which was epitomised by his stunning capture of European Footballer of the Year Kevin Keegan. In June 1985 he quit The Dell to return to his native north-east with Sunderland but it did not work out. In 1990 he became England's assistant manager under Graham Taylor, working with the under-21s. When Taylor quit in November 1993, McMenemy went too but two months later he was back at The Dell as Director of Football to assist Alan Ball, then Dave Merrington and finally Graeme Souness. When Souness abruptly quit because of differences with chairman Rupert Lowe, McMenemy went too. He briefly managed Northern Ireland and continued to work in the media and with his many charities until the ousting of Lowe opened the door for a welcome return. In the absence of a suite named after him, he hosted the Ambassadors Club for two years until the return of Lowe as chairman spelled a third exit for one of the club's legends, who was awarded the MBE for his services to football and charity.

HOME FIRES BURNING

Saints' best ever season at The Dell came in 1975-76 when they won 18 and lost only one of their 21 Division Two games there. But Lawrie McMenemy's men finished only sixth, undone by an away record of 13 defeats and just three wins.

MAGIC MATT

Matthew Le Tissier will surely go down as the greatest player in the club's history, not just for his 209 goals in 462 appearances or for an almost equal number of assists but for his incredible loyalty. This genius could have earned much more elsewhere but stayed to become a one-club man and almost single-handedly kept them in the Premier League even when all seemed lost. Tottenham and Chelsea were among the clubs keen to take him – and perhaps that might have enabled him to win more than the paltry eight England caps which do not do justice to his supreme ability. All his goals were scored at the top level and many were spectacular contenders for the Goal of the Season award in their own right. No wonder fans nicknamed him Le God. His laid-back, nonchalant style belied an incredible talent and steely determination to turn it on, in the right areas. Although not known for his tackling or tracking back, there were few sharper to the ball if there was a sniff of a goalscoring chance. He made his debut as a substitute against Norwich on August 30, 1986 and made his first start three days later in a 2-0 win at home to Tottenham, the side he supported as a boy. His first goals for the club came in a League Cup tie against Manchester United on November 4, 1986. Having come off the bench he netted twice in a 4-1 win which cost Ron Atkinson his job as United boss. Four days later he grabbed his first league goal with a deft lob in a 3-1 defeat at Sheffield Wednesday. He won the Barclays Young Player of the Year award in 1990 and the BBC Goal of the Season trophy for his spectacular 30-yard strike against Blackburn in December 1994 whilst thriving under Alan Ball who built the side around him. The tactics were simple – it was down to the other 10 players to win the ball and give it to Le Tissier who would do the rest! He never won an England under-21 cap but did play for the B team in a final trial match for the 1998 World Cup squad. He scored a hat-trick but was still scandalously overlooked. Fittingly, he scored the last ever league goal at The Dell in true Roy of the Rovers fashion, swivelling to hit an injury-time winner against Arsenal. He received a well deserved testimonial in 2002 after being forced to quit through as series of persistent niggling injuries and is now excellent value as a television pundit. He has a suite at St Mary's and a Flybe plane named after him.

FREEDOM OF THE CITY

Southampton's greatest honour was bestowed upon the football club following the FA Cup win in 1976. Long-serving stalwart Ted Bates was similarly honoured in 2001. Following his retirement in 2002, Matthew Le Tissier also received the Freedom of the City and he was followed in 2008 by former manager Lawrie McMenemy.

VETERAN KEEPER

Len Wilkins continued playing until the ripe old age of 73! The half-back joined Southampton from school and made his debut against Leicester on October 23, 1948. He was a vegetarian long before it became a widely adopted trend, earning him the nickname 'Spud' for his love of potatoes. He could play anywhere in defence and was a natural choice to become team captain. The last of his 275 appearances for the club came at home to Watford in April 1958 and he received a standing ovation from the crowd as he walked to the centre circle to toss the coin. He then emigrated to Canada where he played for Ontario All Stars. He later had stints with three different clubs in California and when the legs no longer carried him through games outfield, he went in goal playing in local leagues until he was 73. He died five years later.

MARSHALL LAW

Scott Marshall played just two games for Saints – and scored in both. Unfortunately both were own goals! He arrived on a Bosman free transfer but with a big reputation having broken into Arsenal's first-team at 19 and making five appearances for the Scotland under-21 side. He had a decent pedigree. His father and brother both played in the Scottish top-flight as goalkeepers while his sister was Scotland's most capped basketball player. Marshall made his debut in a 3-0 defeat at Leeds in September 1998 and was unlucky to turn the ball into his own net. Four days later he did it again this time in a 4-0 defeat at Newcastle. It meant Saints had lost their first five games of the season, their worst ever start to a campaign. Marshall never played for Saints again. He made one appearance on loan at Celtic before moving to Brentford for £250,000 in October 1999.

BRITISH HOLMES STORE

After a career of making news, Nick Holmes found himself selling it following his retirement from the game. After a brief spell on the coaching staff at The Dell, he opened his own village shop in Winterslow, near Salisbury starting work at 6am each morning. He then moved to Florida to run a property management business before returning to England to take the reins at Salisbury City, guiding them from the second tier of the Southern League to the Conference. Holmes was a one-club man, making 535 appearances during his 14 years at The Dell as either a left-back or midfielder. Only Terry Paine and Mike Channon had made more appearances for the club when a pelvic injury forced him to retire in May 1987. Holmes and David Peach are the only two men to have played in two Wembley finals for the club. Born in Woolston, he is widely regarded as one of the best native Southampton players.

SAINTS SIGN CLARKE OF THE COURT

The only player to score a hat-trick on his Southampton debut is Colin Clarke who signed from Bournemouth for £400,000 in July 1986. His impressive displays for Northern Ireland in the 1986 World Cup finals in Mexico prompted Chris Nicholl to bring him the short distance from Dean Court. Clarke netted three in his first game, an opening day 5-0 win at home to QPR. He went on to score 20 goals in that season and 16 the next and also became Northern Ireland's record goalscorer at that time with 13 goals from 38 appearances. However, that also prompted him to angle for a move to a bigger club. After six months of acrimony, he was sold to QPR for £800,000 in March 1989. But he struggled to recapture his goalscoring momentum and moved to Pompey for half that amount in May of the following year. A knee injury forced him to retire and he became a successful coach with FC Dallas in America.

ALL SAINTS DAY

In 2006, Saints decided they would hold a minute's silence before the game nearest to November 1, All Saints Day, in rememberance of former players, staff or fans who had passed away during the previous year.

FOREST FIRES

Two of Saints' four appearances at Wembley have been against Nottingham Forest. After beating Manchester United 1-0 in the 1976 FA Cup Final and losing by the same score in the Charity Shield to Liverpool, Lawrie McMenemy's men returned to the Twin Towers for the 1979 League Cup final. They went 2-0 down in the semi-final at Leeds but fought back to draw 2-2 with goals by Nick Holmes and Steve Williams before winning the second leg at The Dell 1-0 with Terry Curran netting his only goal for the club. There was heavy snow the night before the March 17 final but the pitch was in good condition. Saints took the lead after 17 minutes when David Peach broke onto an Alan Ball pass to fire past Peter Shilton. Southampton led at the interval but Forest hit back with two goals from Gary Birtles and one from Tony Woodcock. Although Holmes pulled one back with a left-foot volley in the last minute, Saints could not quite force extra-time. Saints met Forest again on their next visit to Wembley 13 years later – and with the same scoreline. This time it was the Zenith Data Systems Cup Final on March 29, 1992 in front of 67,688 fans, most it seemed from the south coast. Scot Gemmill and Ian Black put Forest 2-0 up but Matthew Le Tissier headed in a Neil Ruddock cross on 64 minutes. Kevin Moore nodded the equaliser six minutes later but Gemmill nicked it eight minutes from the end of extra-time.

CRUEL FOR KEEGAN

If only the "inactive zone" offside rule had been introduced when Manchester United came to town in December 1981 as Kevin Keegan was robbed of what would have been his greatest ever goal. Saints were level at 2-2 with 16 minutes remaining when the England striker acrobatically hooked a brilliant bicycle volley over his head from 16 yards. It was a stunning strike which would surely have been Goal of the Season but after consulting a linesman, the referee reluctantly ruled it out because David Armstrong was standing in an offside position – although clearly not interfering with play. Some justice was done as Armstrong raced through to give Saints a last-minute winner, one of his 15 goals from midfield that season.

PLAY THROUGH THE PAINE

Saints' record number of appearances is unlikely ever to be broken. Terry Paine made an incredible total of 811 starts, plus four games from the bench, between March 1957 and April 1974. He was spotted playing for Winchester City and had trials at both Pompey and Arsenal before he was signed by Ted Bates who persuaded him to give up his job as a coachbuilder at Eastleigh's British Rail depot. He made just one appearance for the Reserves before being promoted to the senior side where he quickly established himself as a key man. A classy, jinking winger, he had a knack for getting to the byline and landing a cross on the head of a succession of strikers for whom his service was meat and drink. Derek Reeves and George O'Brien were the first to profit, a combination which played a huge part in Southampton's march to the Division Three title in 1960. Paine's impressive form won him the first of 19 England caps in May 1963 – and he was an integral part of Alf Ramey's World Cup winning squad in 1966. However he played just one game in the finals (v Mexico) and it proved to be his last international appearance as the manager opted for a "wingless wonders" formation. Harshly, only the players who played in the final would receive winners medals – an anomaly which was not corrected until 2007 when they were belatedly awarded to the whole squad. In addition to helping England to World Cup glory, Paine had another reason to enjoy 1966 as he headed the vital goal at Leyton Orient to clinch Southampton's place in the top-flight for the first time in their history. Paine continued to supply a stream of crosses, for Martin Chivers and Ron Davies and then for Mike Channon whose fledgling career received a huge boost from the service from the flanks. He finally left the club in 1974 when new boss Lawrie McMenemy set about rebuilding the side. Paine moved to Hereford and took part in a further 106 games to set a new Football League record of 819 appearances – a figure which has since been surpassed by former Saints keeper Peter Shilton, as well as Grimsby striker Tony Ford. His longevity earned him the MBE and after a successful coaching career in South Africa and a brief stint at Coventry, he returned to Johannesburg where he now fronts his own sports show on television. He has a suite named after him at St Mary's with one of his England caps proudly on display.

WIDE OF THE MARK

As predictions go it was right up there with life on the Moon, the Millennium bug and advice to "Buy, Buy, Buy!" on Black Wednesday! After selling Alan Shearer to Blackburn for a British record £3.6m (and no sell-on clause!) in July 1992, manager Ian Branfoot replaced him with Kerry Dixon and David Speedie, and promised fans they would outscore Shearer. The duo, who has forged such a good partnership in their prime at Chelsea, were now past their best. While Shearer banged in goals with awesome regularity, Speedie and Dixon managed just two between them. Both made just 12 appearances for the club with Dixon netting at Liverpool and Leeds. Speedie had been thrown in as a make-weight in the deal with Blackburn. Branfoot really wanted Mike Newell but Saints caved in – and Speedie made it clear he did not fancy the move either. Immediately after a 2-1 home defeat by QPR, Branfoot took the team to Jersey for a "bonding" trip which went disastrously wrong. A clear-the-air meeting in the bar became increasingly heated as players gave their opinions and vented their frustration. It ended in uproar when Speedie hit Micky Adams over the head with an ashtray, his defence being that he was aiming for Terry Hurlock! He flew home early while the rest of the squad stayed on for the rest of a "goodwill" visit which saw them beat a Jersey Select XI 4-1 with two goals from Nicky Banger and one each from Hurlock and Matthew Le Tissier. Speedie was loaned to Birmingham, West Brom and West Ham before signing for Leicester in August 1993. Dixon was twice loaned to his home-town club Luton who made the move permanent in October 1993.

WORLD CUP STARS

Two World Cup finalists have gone on to manage Saints. Alan Ball gave a man-of-the-match display in midfield to help England to a 4-2 win over West Germany in 1966 under the charge of former Saints full-back Alf Ramsey. Ball went on to boss Southampton from February 1994 until July 1995. Jan Poortvliet played full-back for Holland in their 3-1 defeat by hosts Argentina in 1978. He took over as Head Coach at St Mary's in June 2008.

ALAN BALL

DOZEN GOAL RUSH

In December 1966, Saints Reserves beat Reading Reserves 8-4 at The Dell with all 12 goals coming in the first 68 minutes.

SOUTHAMPTON ST MARY'S

Southampton Football Club was formed in November 1885 as Southampton St Mary's Young Men's Association. However, as four of the founding members had also formed Deanery FC five years earlier, it could be argued that the club's roots go back even further. Rev Arthur Sole of St Mary's Church convened a meeting in Grove Street, just behind the church. The main item on the agenda was to discuss which type of football they would play - Association or Rugby. Thankfully they went with the former after a lengthy debate. Rev Sole became the president, AA Fry the first captain and Mr C Abbott the secretary. They played their first game on November 21, 1885 beating Freemantle 5-1 on a pitch in Northlands Road. The YMA part of the club name was dropped three years later and in 1897 a limited company was formed with the title Southampton Football and Athletic Company Ltd. The club returned to its roots in 2001, building their new ground just round the corner from the meeting hall where they had been formed. Initially it was named the Friends Provident Stadium but following uproar from the fans this was changed to the Friends Provident St Mary's Stadium. When Flybe succeeded Friends Provident as main sponsors in 2005, they declined the naming rights and the ground became known simply as the St Mary's Stadium.

ONE FOR THE ROAD

During the first half of the 1996-97 season whenever Saints played away, the opposition goalkeeper could have gone home just as soon as he had conceded a goal. In the first 13 games of the campaign, Graeme Souness' side scored exactly once in every away league game – regardless of whether they won, lost or drew. The run was finally broken on March 12 when Saints drew 0-0 against Leeds United at Elland Road.

DEL BOY

Agustin Delgado became the first Ecuadorian international to play in the Premiership – although it is still unclear who actually signed him! The deal was set up during the last days of Stuart Gray's reign as manager but completed just as he was replaced by Gordon Strachan in November 2001. Certainly it was one of the club's more disappointing transfers. Great things were expected of the £3.5m signing from Mexican side Necaxa but despite occasional flashes of his talent, he failed to live up to his build-up. His impressive tally of 29 goals in 43 internationals included a winner against Brazil to help seal his country's first ever appearance at the World Cup finals but his commitment to his new club never matched that to his country. He arrived at St Mary's nursing a knee injury which required surgery, delaying his debut until January 13, 2002 when he came off the bench to replace the injured James Beattie in a 3-1 home defeat by Manchester United. He showed flashes of ability but then failed to shine in an FA Cup shock defeat on a bitterly cold night at Rotherham after the initial tie had been postponed because of a frozen pitch. His entire focus seemed to be on getting fit for the World Cup finals – under strict instructions from the country's president. After further surgery, he played all three games for Ecuador in Japan, and became the first Southampton player ever to score in the World Cup finals when he netted a header against Mexico. That put huge stress on his troublesome knee and unbeknown to the club, he then had further surgery back in Ecuador which ruled him out until the autumn. He returned to help Saints beat leaders Arsenal 3-2, winning a penalty and then scoring the decisive goal. He followed that up with a smartly-taken goal in a League Cup tie at Liverpool, but then suffered a recurrence of his knee problem. It seemed he was continually in dispute with the club, even threatening to quit Southampton because the club forgot his birthday! That prompted Strachan to go round to every player at the training ground to wish them a happy birthday for that year! He also claimed he was unfit to play because of teeth problems and then developed a back injury. Fed up at persistent media questions about Delgado, Strachan famously said he had more important things to worry about, like a yoghurt on its sell-by date! Eventually Saints were forced to cut their losses and allow him to return home for a fraction of the massive outlay. Even more annoying was the fact he then seemed to recapture fitness and form!

THE MARIAN KIND

Marian Pahars became the first Latvian to play in the Premiership when he signed for Saints in March 1999. The diminutive striker had impressed in a trial match for the Reserves, scoring a hat-trick to persuade Dave Jones to sign him. However, the move from Skonto Riga was held up by red tape as the PFA objected to the application for a work permit. After a concerted campaign, Saints won the appeal and the move was completed hours before the transfer deadline. Pahars arrived without even a pair of proper boots to his name and was preparing to sew repairs to his old ones until he was given the money to go and buy some new ones! He repaid the club with some vital goals, most notably a double in the final-day 2-0 win over Everton to ensure Saints stayed up. Arriving with a reputation as Latvia's answer to Michael Owen, he soon established himself as one of the most dangerous strikers in the Premiership with his pace, quick feet and eye for goal. He was joined at the club by compatriot Imants Bleidelis whose cause was not helped by the departure of manager Dave Jones who had set up the deal. Bleidelis struggled to impress new boss Glenn Hoddle and left the club by mutual consent in January 2003, signing for Viborg in Denmark. Pahars and Bleidelis both played for Latvia in the finals of Euro 2004 and a recurring ankle problem meant Pahars did not have his contract renewed in May 2006.

RUNNERS-UP AND RELEGATED

In 2006, Saints finished second in the FA Premier Reserve League (South) but found themselves relegated to the Pontins Holidays Combination League. A re-structuring meant that only top-flight clubs could participate in the FA Premier Reserve League and as Southampton had been relegated the previous year, they were excluded.

BRIDGE TOO FAR

When Wayne Bridge limped off after 79 minutes of the 1-0 home defeat by Liverpool on January 18, 2003, it brought to an end his astonishing run of 10,160 consecutive minutes of league football – a Premiership record for an outfield player.

SIDE BY SYD

While Terry Paine took most of the plaudits as Saints won promotion from Divisions 3 and then 2 to reach the top-flight, the contribution of John Sydenham was equally important on the opposite flank. Less tricky but faster than Paine, Sydenham set up a regular stream of chances – including three of Ron Davies' four goals at Old Trafford. He probably retired too early and emigrated to Australia to set up his own insurance consultancy. He regularly returns to visit the club he played for from 1957 until 1970, scoring 40 goals in 401 appearances.

JINX BROKEN

Saints broke a long hoodoo as they twice came from behind to force a fine 3-2 victory at Burnley on September 23, 2006. It was 12 years almost to the day since they had previously come from 1-0 down to win away from home in the league with a 3-1 victory at Coventry on September 24, 1994. The only other occasion they had come from behind to win away in that time was when they trailed 2-1 after taking the lead at Chelsea on New Year's Day 2002 but hit back to win 4-2.

YOU'RE ALRIGHT JACK

The club's north-east scout Jack Hixon proved an invaluable resource discovering midfielders George Shipley, Neil Maddison, Tommy Widdrington, defender Steve Davis and future England striker Alan Shearer, among others.

REID AND RIGHT

After Peter Reid was sacked as manager at Manchester City, Ian Branfoot persuaded him to pull on his boots once more and join Southampton on a short-term contract. With Saints in crisis and the boss under pressure, many felt that Branfoot had hastened his inevitable departure by bringing in his own successor. But Reid insisted on a clause in his contract stating he would not take the job if it became available; he did not want to be accused of stabbing the boss in the back. After eight good games, he left The Dell shortly before Branfoot was axed.

CHANNON FODDER

Mike Channon is the club's record goalscorer with 228 goals from 602 appearances in a Saints shirt. With Matthew Le Tissier forced into retirement still 19 goals short of Channon's total, it is a record which is unlikely to be broken in the very near future. However, the deal very nearly didn't happen as Saints just pipped Swindon to the signature of the Wiltshire Schools hot-shot in March 1964. Rival boss Bert Head had arranged to meet Channon on a Monday with a view to getting him to sign for the Robins. Saints manager Ted Bates was tipped off by the boss of Channon's club side at youth level. Bates went to the youngster's house 24 hours before Head was due to visit and stole a march by signing him up initially on amateur forms in order to avoid breaking the FA rule which prevented clubs from signing players as professionals on a Sunday! At 15 years and 10 months, he was then the youngest player ever to play for Saints Reserves – a record later broken by Andrew Surman. His direct running and eye for goal soon saw him promoted to the first-team allowing Bates to sell Martin Chivers to Spurs, safe in the knowledge he had a ready-made replacement in Channon. The forward quickly struck up a great rapport on the field with both Ron Davies and Terry Paine and off the field with the Saints supporters. Despite being a target for almost every top club in the country, he remained loyal to Southampton even after the club's relegation from the First Division in 1974. He was rewarded with an FA Cup winners medal two years later but then joined Manchester City in July 1977 for £300,000. The move did not work out and Channon was delighted when Lawrie McMenemy brought him back to The Dell in September 1979 where he immediately regained his goalscoring form forging a strong partnership, first with Phil Boyer and then with Kevin Keegan. After 185 league goals, his famous 'windmill' arm-whirling celebration was seen for the last time on April 24, 1982 when he rounded off a flowing move involving virtually the entire team to make it 1-1 in a 3-2 home defeat by Liverpool. He scored 20 goals in 46 appearances for England, all but one of his caps earned as a Southampton player. He has a suite named after him at St Mary's and is now established as a hugely successful racehorse trainer.

LEADING MARKSMEN (LEAGUE)

Matthew Le Tissier finished as Saints' leading marksman in the league eight times in nine seasons. Mike Channon topped the club's goalscoring charts for seven successive seasons from 1969-70 after Ron Davies had done three times in a row.

Season	Player	Goals (Total games)
2007-08	Stern John	19 (46 Championship games)
2006-07	Grzegorz Rasiak	18 (46 Championship games)
2005-06	Ricardo Fuller	9 (46 Championship games)
2004-05	Peter Crouch	12 (38 Premiership games)
2003-04	James Beattie	14 (38 Premiership games)
2002-03	James Beattie	23 (38 Premiership games)
2001-02	Marian Pahars	14 (38 Premiership games)
2000-01	James Beattie	11 (38 Premiership games)
1999-00	Marian Pahars	13 (38 Premiership games)
1998-99	Egil Ostenstad	7 (38 Premiership games)
1997-98	Egil Ostenstad	11 (38 Premiership games)
	Matthew Le Tissier	11 (38 Premiership games)
1996-97	Matthew Le Tissier	13 (38 Premiership games)
1995-96	Matthew Le Tissier	7 (38 Premiership games)
	Neil Shipperley	7 (38 Premiership games)
1994-95	Matthew Le Tissier	20 (42 Premiership games)
1993-94	Matthew Le Tissier	25 (42 Premiership games)
1992-93	Matthew Le Tissier	15 (42 Premiership games)
1991-92	Alan Shearer	13 (42 Division One games)
1990-91	Matthew Le Tissier	19 (38 Division One games)
1989-90	Matthew Le Tissier	20 (38 Division One games)
1988-89	Rod Wallace	12 (38 Division One games)
1987-88	Colin Clarke	16 (40 Division One games)
1986-87	Colin Clarke	20 (42 Division One games)
1985-86	David Armstrong	10 (42 Division One games)
1984-85	Joe Jordan	12 (42 Division One games)
1983-84	Steve Moran	21 (42 Division One games)
1982-83	Danny Wallace	12 (42 Division One games)
1981-82	Kevin Keegan	26 (42 Division One games)
1980-81	Steve Moran	18 (42 Division One games)

1979-80 ...... Phil Boyer .... 23 (42 Division One games)
1978-79 ...... Nick Holmes .... 8 (42 Division One games)
1977-78 ...... Phil Boyer .... 17 (42 Division Two games)
1976-77 ...... Ted MacDougall .... 23 (42 Division Two games)
1975-76 ...... Mike Channon .... 20 (42 Division Two games)
1974-75 ...... Mike Channon .... 20 (42 Division Two games)
1973-74 ...... Mike Channon .... 21 (42 Division One games)
1972-73 ...... Mike Channon .... 16 (42 Division One games)
1971-72 ...... Mike Channon .... 14 (42 Division One games)
1970-71 ...... Mike Channon .... 18 (42 Division One games)
1969-70 ...... Mike Channon .... 15 (42 Division One games)
1968-69 ...... Ron Davies .... 20 (42 Division One games)
1967-68 ...... Ron Davies .... 28 (42 Division One games)
1966-67 ...... Ron Davies .... 37 (42 Division One games)

END OF AN ERA

Before their relegation in 2005, Saints were the fifth-longest surviving top-flight club; they were relegated after 27 years in the First Division, which in 1992 became the Premier League. Only Arsenal, Everton, Manchester United and Liverpool had been in the top division for longer.

Saints' historical league status

1894-1920........................ Southern League
1920 .... Division Three
1921-22.................. Division Three (South)
promoted as champions
1922-53................................. Division Two
1953-58.................. Division Three (South)
1958-60 .... Division Three
promoted as champions
1960-1966.............................. Division Two
1966-1974.............................. Division One
1974-1978.............................. Division Two
1978-1992.............................. Division One
1992-2005.................. FA Premier League
2005-present .... FL Championship

THANK EVANS

Saints looked to be heading for relegation until they signed striker Micky Evans in March 1997. It was £500,000 well spent as he scored four goals in eight appearances to fire the side to safety. When they went to fellow strugglers Nottingham Forest on April 5, Southampton were bottom of the table, three points adrift of Forest and seven away from safety. Travelling to the game, the team were shocked to hear a preview writing them off saying they had already taken one relegation place. Evans broke clear one-on-one to score twice in the last five minutes and earn his side a vital 3-1 win. His battling approach was best summed up in the vital six-pointer at home to West Ham a week later. It was a crunch game Saints simply had to win against their fellow strugglers. After 12 minutes Robbie Slater slung in a cross from the left towards the far post where Evans was charging in full tilt. From such a tight angle, the only way he could possibly score was by colliding with the post and without a thought for his own safety, Evans hurtled into the woodwork and squeezed home the header. He was unable to celebrate as he lay unconscious in the goalmouth. Saints won 2-0 and stayed up with Evans recovering from his knock to net again in the next game, a 2-2 draw at home to Coventry. That won him the Premiership Player of the Month award for April but the arrival of Kevin Davies meant his chances became limited. He won a solitary cap for the Republic of Ireland against Romania just days before a £750,000 move to West Brom in October 1997.

RIDEOUT OF REACH

Paul Rideout played for Hampshire and Southampton Schools as a youngster but turned down Saints as a 16-year-old because he didn't like the way he'd been treated. Instead he joined Swindon, and then Aston Villa and Bari before finally arriving at The Dell for £350,000. He scored 21 goals in 87 appearances before Ian Branfoot sold him to Notts County for £300,000 – due to the emergence of Alan Shearer. Rideout proved he was far from finished and had successful spells at Glasgow Rangers and Everton, scoring the only goal in the 1995 FA Cup Final against Manchester United. He then had two spells in China, and another in the USA before joining Tranmere, for whom he hit a hat-trick in that epic FA Cup fifth round replay which saw Rovers beat Saints 4-3.

GRAY DAY FOR SAINTS

Stuart Gray took an unlikely route to the manager's job at Southampton. Signed from Aston Villa for £200,000 in 1991, he made just 20 appearances before a serious Achilles injury forced him to hang up his boots. His solitary goal came in an FA Cup tie at Old Trafford which Saints won on penalties after a 2-2 draw. He joined The Dell backroom staff in a coaching capacity and his talents soon earned him a role at Wolves as reserve team coach – and briefly as caretaker boss. However his family were unable to settle in the area, and he returned to Southampton. With no coaching vacancies, he was appointed as the club's community officer until Dave Jones appointed him as reserve team coach in July 1997. He stepped up to become first-team coach 17 months later and continued in that role under Glenn Hoddle before taking over from him in a caretaker role in March 2001. He was confirmed as manager in his own right in June of the same year and took charge of the club as they moved to their new home at St Mary's. But they struggled to settle into their new surroundings, not helped by a bad run of injuries and results. He was sacked in November 2001 but quickly found another job as a coach at Aston Villa, taking over as caretaker boss once more when John Gregory was sacked. He again lost his job when Graham Taylor was axed but found success as boss of Northampton Town.

RECORD KEEPERS

Saints are fortunate to have four committed historians to chart and chronicle the story of the club from its humble beginnings to the modern day. David Bull, Gary Chalk, Duncan Holley and Dave Juson founded a publishing company, opting for the fitting title of Hagiology, which means the study of saints. They have published five books to date, most notably *In That Number* which is essential for any Southampton supporter – as well as this author! An astonishingly comprehensive statistical tome, it contains details of every post-war game, competitive, friendly or reserve. *Match of the Millennium* goes into greater detail on 100 selected games while *Full-time at The Dell* tells the story of the club's old ground and the move to St Mary's. *Saints v Pompey* does what it says on the tin and *Dell Diamond* is a biography of Ted Bates. Next in the pipeline is the biography of Terry Paine.

MR SOUTHAMPTON

Ted Bates signed for Saints from Norwich on his 19th birthday – and stayed for 66 years! Then known as Eddie, he soon forced his way into the first-team – until the war put his career on hold. Returning to Southampton after demob, he struck up a powerful striking partnership with Charlie Wayman, netting 63 goals in 202 league appearances. He hung up his boots in 1952 and, having already taken on some coaching duties, was put in charge of the Reserves. He was appointed as manager in September 1955 and led the team out of the Third Division (South) in 1960 with the team storming to promotion with an exciting array of talent which included the youthful Terry Paine and John Sydenham. Six years later he led the club into the top division for the first time in their history and – despite selling Martin Chivers to Spurs for a British record £125,000 – he kept them there with some astute signings including Ron Davies, Jimmy Gabriel and John McGrath who were brought in for nominal amounts plus Mike Channon who was spotted playing for Wiltshire Schools. In 1969, he led the club into Europe for the first time as they qualified for the Fairs Cup barely nine years after escaping the third tier of English football. He established his beloved Saints as a strong force in the top division until – after 865 games in charge – he seamlessly handed over the reins to Lawrie McMenemy who was to build on the foundations Bates had laid. Ted's knowledge and experience were too valuable to lose and he stayed on: first as chief executive and then as director, and finally as club president. Known almost universally as Mr Southampton, he was awarded an MBE and the Freedom of the City in 2001 when he also officially opened the new St Mary's Stadium along with Matthew Le Tissier. He passed away on November 26, 2003 but his guiding hand will forever be felt at the club and an annual trophy has been set up in his memory.

RELEGATING RIVALS

Three days after securing their place in the 1976 FA Cup final, Saints celebrated in style with a 1-0 win at Pompey thanks to a last-minute goal by Mike Channon. Not only did it complete a second successive double over their local rivals but it also condemned the Fratton Park club to relegation.

JOHN MORTI-MORE

John Mortimore is now in his third and longest spell at the club. After a successful playing career with Chelsea from 1956 to 1965, he moved into coaching, joining Saints as assistant manager in March 1968, beating future boss Lawrie McMenemy to the post. He left Saints in the summer of 1971 to join Ethnikos of Greece and then Benfica. He won the Portuguese championship in his first season and finished second in the following two years. He returned to Southampton in 1979 as assistant manager to Lawrie McMenemy and remained at the club until 1985 when he was tempted back to Benfica, where he won two more Portuguese cup finals and one league title, before moving to Real Betis of Spain. He again returned to Saints as assistant manager and chief scout in 1989 and took on the ambassadorial role of club president when Ted Bates sadly passed away in November 2003.

STAY-UP POMPEY

Saints saved south coast rivals Portsmouth from relegation in April 1965 when Ted Bates' side won their final Division Two fixture 2-1 at Swindon to relegate them. A draw would have been enough to send Pompey down in their place on goal average. The favour was not returned 40 years later when Pompey lost at West Brom to help send Southampton into the Championship.

PUT IN PERSPECTIVE

Saints won 2-1 at West Ham on April 15, 1989 thanks to goals by Rod Wallace and Paul Rideout – but the result paled into insignificance as news filtered through of the terrible disaster at Hillsborough, where 96 Liverpool fans were tragically crushed to death at the FA Cup semi-final between the Reds and Nottingham Forest. The Taylor report blamed fences and police control that led to the introduction of all-seater stadia. Saints were forced to reconstruct the Milton Road and Archers Road ends of The Dell cutting their capacity to a paltry 15,200 which was clearly unsustainable in the Premier League.

THERE'S ONLY TWO RON DAVIES

Saints fans were unable to sing "There's only one Ron Davies" as the club had two of them! The best known of course is Ron Tudor Davies who scored 153 goals in 277 appearances, including a four-goal haul at Old Trafford in August 1969. The other was Ron Thomas Davies who played 192 games at full-back between March 1958 and August 1964. Ted Bates spent £7,000 to bring him to The Dell from Cardiff and he was pretty much a regular in the side until the arrival of Stuart Williams prompted him to move to Aldershot.

PLYMOUTH COME UNSTUCK

In November 1958, Plymouth arrived at The Dell six points clear at the top of Division Three prompting their supporters to plaster the city centre with stickers boasting "Argyle for Division Two". Saints punished them with a thumping 5-1 win with two goals from Terry Paine and one each from Derek Reeves, Don Roper and John Sydenham. However the Pilgrims progressed to Division Two as champions while Saints were left stuck in 14th place.

SAME AGAIN

Saints were unchanged for nine successive matches (seven league and two cup) from October 16, 1954 to December 11, 1954. They won five and drew one in the league and won an FA Cup tie 4-1 at Barnet before losing at Grimsby in the second round to finally prompt a change of line-up. The starting XI was: Kiernan, Turner, Traynor, McLaughlin, Wilkins, Simpson, Flood, Mulgrew, Day, Walker, Hoskins.

LEAKING GOALS

Saints won the Division Three title in 1960 – despite conceding a record 75 goals! No team had ever previously won that division (regional or otherwise) conceding more than 70. However, that was outweighed by the 106 goals they scored with striker Derek Reeves bagging 39 of them – twice as many as his nearest rival George O'Brien.

SURLY SARLI

The wonderfully-named Italian striker Cosimo Sarli scored eight goals in the first four Reserve games of the 1998-99 season to have fans clamouring for him to be given a chance in the first-team. But he failed to maintain the momentum and after a brief and unsuccessful spell with Belgian side Aalst, he ended up rejoining his former club Nitra FC scoring once in four games before signing for Nice where he netted twice in 14 appearances in 1999-2000. He then had two seasons at Crotone hitting three goals in 23 games before rediscovering his touch at Montichiari where he netted 11 in 12 games. However his form deserted him at Aglianese where he failed to pot in 12 matches. He went back to Montichiari and grabbed two in 11 and then hit four in 10 back at Aglianese before moving to Legnano where he bagged five in 25. He went back to Montichiari but could not prevent them being relegated to Serie D in 2006-07.

SEEING RED

Nicknamed Fusey because of his short temper, Micky Adams became the first Saints player to be sent off in the Premier League – in only the club's second game in the competition. The fiery full-back was dismissed in the last minute of a 3-1 defeat at QPR on August 19, 1992, for an off-the-ball incident spotted by the referee. The first player to be sent off after the club joined the Football League was Jimmy Moore in a home defeat by Grimsby in December 1920.

SURVEYING HIS CAREER

While playing for Saints, Kevin Moore became a qualified chartered surveyor and used his qualification after hanging up his boots to become Fulham's safety officer and then their training ground manager. He signed from Oldham for £150,000 in July 1987, less than six months after arriving at Boundary Park from Grimsby where he had been a team-mate of Southampton boss Chris Nicholl. He had a clause in his contract allowing him to leave if a First Division club came calling and he made 180 appearances for Saints, scoring 13 goals including the equaliser in the 1992 Zenith Data Systems Cup Final at Wembley.

FOURTEEN FINAL DAY FLOPS

Saints had a dreadful run of 14 successive seasons where they failed to win their last match of the campaign. After a Steve Moran double and a goal from David Armstrong gave them a 3-1 victory at Notts County to clinch second spot in Division One in 1984, they then failed to win their final fixture until 1999 when they beat Wimbledon with goals by Marian Pahars and Wayne Bridge. The result relegated the Dons.

Season	Opponents	Score
1997-98	Spurs (a)	1-1
1996-97	Aston Villa (a)	0-1
1995-96	Wimbledon (h)	0-0
1994-95	Leicester City (h)	2-2
1993-94	West Ham United (a)	3-3
1992-93	Oldham Athletic (a)	3-4
1991-92	Arsenal (a)	1-5
1990-91	Wimbledon (h)	1-1
1989-90	Spurs (a)	1-2
1988-89	Millwall (a)	1-1
1987-88	Luton Town (h)	1-1
1986-87	Coventry City (a)	1-1
1985-86	Spurs (a)	3-5
1984-85	Liverpool (h)	1-1

RAF JUSTICE

Peter Sillett missed the 1953 FA Cup third round replay at home to Lincoln because the RAF wanted him for the semi-final of its Inter-Command Championship. The RAF side went on to reach the final which clashed with an FA Cup fifth round tie at home to mighty Blackpool: Stanley Matthews and all. This time Sillett was released to the relief of Tommy Traynor who had stepped in the first time. Saints led at half-time through John Walker but were hit by two in four minutes after the break to go down 2-1. Blackpool went on to Wembley where they beat Bolton 4-3 in what is still known as the Matthews Final.

KILLER CAPTURED

Saints paid French club Troyes £2m in July 2002 for Michael Svensson, and he arrived with the nickname 'Killer' – due to his ruthless approach to the game. He began his career with Swedish club Halmstad where team-mates gave him the tag, having been on the end of some crunching training ground tackles. A commanding centre-back, he was an instant success and played a major role in the club's run to the 2003 FA Cup final. He was sorely missed in the relegation season after picking up a bad knee injury in March 2004 which ruled him out of the Euro 2004 finals for Sweden. The original injury occurred in 1997 when he damaged posterior cruciate ligaments but managed to play on without a reconstruction. But seven years later he began feeling sharp pain and needed two operations. He retruned to playing in late 2005 and managed eight Championship appearances before breaking down again. He had further surgery and visited specialists in Germany for treatment which proved unsuccessful. Virtually everyone told him he would never play again but Svensson refused to accept defeat and organised his own operation. In March 2007 cartilage was removed and grown in a lab before being replaced two months later when he also underwent a reconstruction. Although his contract had expired, Saints continued to give him support and helped him along the lonely road to recovery. Showing enormous determination, he somehow battled back through a year of rehab. He researched it himself and booked into a clinic in Bologna where three spells of treatment appeared to achieve the elusive breakthrough. To the delight of all Saints fans, he resumed playing in pre-season 2008, played in a testimonial for pal and defensive partner Claus Lundekvam, and was named captain for the opening fixture at Cardiff.

TAYLOR-MADE

A delighted Maik Taylor signed for Southampton in January 1997. Born in Germany to an army family, he was a Saints fan as a schoolboy. He too joined the forces and played for the Army, Farnborough and Basingstoke Town before joining Barnet in June 1995. Graeme Souness paid £500,000 to bring him to The Dell and the six foot four keeper became an instant hit with the fans. However, he lost his place after Dave Jones took over as manager and paid £1m for Paul Jones, recouping most of that outlay by selling Taylor to Fulham for £800,000.

WORLDWIDE SAINTS

Southampton fans are spread worldwide with affiliated supporters groups as far away as Australia and New Zealand, Canada, Singapore and South Africa. However, there is currently no single Supporters Club. The nearest thing to it is the Saints Trust which was formed to give fans better representation to the board.

DISABLED ACCESS

Like most fans, the disabled suffered at The Dell through cramped conditions. But the move to St Mary's enabled the club to introduce good facilities for the disabled and the blind. The stadium has 59 upper tier wheelchair spaces, 117 lower tier wheelchair places, 88 seats for ambulant disabled and 115 seats for the visually impaired with radios and headsets providing commentary from Hospital Broadcasting.

GIRL POWER

Southampton women's team won the FA Cup eight times during the late seventies when they were a real force in the game. They were inspired and driven by Sue Lopez who played 22 times for England from 1972 to 1982 and who was signed by Roma as the first English woman to play semi-professional football and was one of the first two women to gain the FA Advanced Coaching Licence in 1991. After being named Sunday Times Coach of the Year, Sue was awarded the MBE in 2000 for services to women's football.

POPPY POWER

When Saints played away to Leicester on November 5, 2005, the players wore shirts specially embroidered with poppies for Remembrance Day. The shirts were signed and auctioned off in aid of the Royal British Legion's annual poppy appeal. Theo Walcott's shirt was the biggest seller going for £1,251 and the following year Gareth Bale's shirt fetched £877. In 2007, Bradley Wright-Phillips' shirt was the top seller at £404. In total the club has raised almost £20,000 for the servicemen's charity in this way.

LIGHTS OUT

Saints were the last team to play Sunderland under lights at their famous Roker Park Ground before the move to the Stadium of Light. It was a crunch relegation six-pointer coming just three games from the end of the 1996-97 season. Both sides were battling against the drop – and the losers would almost certainly go down. And so it proved. It was a match strictly for those who like their meat raw! Sunderland laid siege to the Southampton goal but Graeme Souness' side stood strong and won it 1-0 with a breakaway goal on 22 minutes, Egil Ostenstad controlling neatly to steer an Alan Neilson cross past Lionel Perez. The Wearsiders finished third from bottom and were relegated just a point behind the Saints!

MISSING THEIR TOUCH

Saints fell behind after just 16 seconds of their Coca-Cola Championship game at Barnsley on December 29, 2007 – without even touching the ball. From kick-off, the Tykes played the ball out to the right for Jamal Campbell-Ryce to send over a cross which held up in the strong swirling wind. Former Saints trainee Brian Howard had run too far forward but managed to stretch and head back for Sam Togwell whose 18-yard volley caught in the wind and sailed into the top right corner before a Southampton player had got a touch. Campbell-Ryce stretched the lead on 33 minutes with a thunderbolt shot to give the home side a 2-0 lead but with the wind in their favour, Saints turned the game around after the break. Two goals from substitute Bradley Wright-Phillips earned a 2-2 draw.

FINISHING HOW THEY STARTED

Saints began and ended the 1963-64 season with 6-1 wins. Charlton were spanked with six of the best in August 1963 with George Kirby grabbing four goals backed up by singles from Stuart Williams and George O'Brien. They finished the campaign in equally emphatic style beating Rotherham with a hat-trick from O'Brien, a double from Terry Paine and one from David Burnside to end up fifth in Division Two.

ORIENT EXPRESS

Having clinched their place in the top-flight with a 1-1 draw at Orient, it was a good omen for Saints as they went back to Brisbane Road – again needing a point for promotion in April 1978. Once again it was a 1-1 draw, once again they came from behind to level with a header, and once again it all but mathematically sealed their place in Division One. An estimated 12,000 Saints fans made the journey and celebrated wildly as Tony Funnell's 39th-minute header cancelled out a Fisher opener. Only Brighton could stop Southampton who were seven goals better off. In their final fixture, Lawrie McMenemy's side hosted Tottenham who also needed a point to be certain of promotion ahead of Brighton. Seagulls supporters may have suspected a carve-up as the game duly ended 0-0 to ensure both sides went up but that was far from the whole story. Saints would have pipped Bolton to the title if they had won so there was no way they were going to take it easy. It was more tense than exciting with Funnell shaving a post as both sides claimed promotion.

Second Division

	P	W	D	L	F	A	Pts
Bolton Wanderers	42	24	10	8	63	33	58
Southampton	42	22	13	7	70	39	57
Tottenham Hotspur	42	20	16	6	83	49	56
Brighton & Hove Albion	42	22	12	8	63	38	56
Blackburn Rovers	42	16	13	13	56	60	45